PUBLIC ADMINISTRATION

PUBLIC ADMINISTRATION

Key Issues Challenging Practitioners

Michael Anthony Tarallo

authorHOUSE®

AuthorHouse™
1663 Liberty Drive
Bloomington, IN 47403
www.authorhouse.com
Phone: 1-800-839-8640

Published by AuthorHouse 4/4/2012

ISBN: 978-1-4685-5970-5 (e)
ISBN: 978-1-4685-5971-2 (hc)
ISBN: 978-1-4685-5972-9 (sc)

Library of Congress Control Number: 2012906012

This book is printed on acid-free paper.

To my wife, children, and family

TABLE OF CONTENTS

Abstract   ix

1. **Introduction**   1

2. **Policy Agenda**   7
   Policy cycle   7
   Making it to the policy agenda   8
   Technical setting   9
   Political setting   12
   Concluding remarks   15

3. **Policy Transfer**   17
   Principles   18
   Opportunities and limitations   19
   Concluding remarks   26

4. **Goal Displacement**   27
   Causes, consequences, and inevitability   28
   Concluding remarks   35

5. **Agencification**   37
   Driving factors   38
   Effectiveness   40
   Concluding remarks   45

6. **Decentralization**   47
   Theoretical frameworks   48
   Accountability   49
   Corruption   52
   Effectiveness   54
   Concluding remarks   56

7. Corruption   **57**

Definition, causes, and consequences   57

Theories on combating corruption   59

Theories that work in practice   61

Concluding remarks   65

8. Public Resources   **67**

Money matters   67

Transparency   69

Public budgeting   72

Public expenditure management   75

Concluding remarks   77

Endnotes   79

References   95

About the Author   111

ABSTRACT

How public affairs are run depends upon the degree of authority and control central government decides to relinquish to regional and local governments, and the extent to which it favors citizen involvement in the governing process. Public administrators do not operate in a vacuum. The context within which decision-making takes place greatly influences public administrators' approach to public issues. Consequently, what government decides to do and how it decides to carry it out affects the lives of people and how people perceive their role in the unfolding of public affairs.

While public administration varies from one country to another, public administrators inevitably face similar challenges. Running a government is not easy; it is complex, dynamic, contested, supported, subject to special interests, both demand- and supply-driven, just to name a few. In executing government functions, public administrators unsurprisingly contend with major decision-making questions. While obviously not exhaustive, this book addresses some key issues challenging practitioners. These challenges include questions on what gets included in the policy agenda, questions on policy response to problems through adoption and/or adaptation of exogenous policies, questions on the dangers of displacing policy goals, questions on transferring government activities to specialized agency, questions on decentralizing powers to regional and local governments, questions on combating corruption, and questions on managing public resources.

It is widely recognized that policy implementation is much more challenging than its design. Nonetheless, it is the manner in which public administrators address these challenges that creates opportunities for a more effective long-term policy prioritization, design and coordination, a more effective and inclusive public governance, and a more effective use of public resources for the delivery of needed public services.

michael anthony

tarallo

Chapter One

Introduction

How public affairs are run depends upon the degree of authority and control central government decides to relinquish to regional and local governments, and the extent to which it favors citizen involvement in the governing process. Public administrators do not operate in a vacuum. The context within which decision making takes place greatly influences public administrators' approach to public issues. Consequently, what government decides to do and how it decides to carry it out affects the lives of people and how people perceive their role in the unfolding of public affairs.

In *Valuing People: Citizen Engagement in Policy Making and Public Service Delivery in Rural Asia* (2012)[1], I argue, echoing what many scholars sustain, that it is by creating an environment where citizens are given democratic space to exercise '*voice*' that government can truly reflect the will of the people, even in between elections. While the institutionalization of the electoral mechanism is by all means a fundamental pillar of democratic society, it is certainly not enough. Despite its merits, in fact, the mechanism falls short of truly empowering and engaging citizens in the decision-making process in matters that matter to the people rather than the elected representatives alone. But can citizen engagement fare well in a country where basic public institutional systems are not fully developed? Or is it the reverse case – can citizen involvement, instead, bring about functional public administration systems? What are really the core principles of the more recent democratic awakening we have witnessed around the world just in the last year? Are the 'awakened' people calling for a change *of* and *in* government with better run institutions and better provided public services alone or are they really demanding to have a direct say, a voice, in decision-making in *addition* to just voting in elected officials? The events represent a great opportunity for citizen engagement; anything less, however, would constitute a half-baked solution. Even if government is better run and public services are provided more efficiently, where does that leave the ordinary person? Are elections and more efficient governments alone truly reflective of the spirit of democracy? When do ordinary individuals cease to be regarded as *customers*, recipient of services, and when do they begin being *citizens*, co-designers of services needed? This is exactly what sets Public Value Management abysmally apart from the New Public Management philosophy in running government and public administrations. Just as individuals can and, more importantly, should be more engaged in public affairs, even government needs to see it this way. In fact, it is certainly up to the government to create an environment where ordinary citizen can play an influential role in decision-making both at the policy level and the delivery of public services.

While government remains central to society, scholars and practitioners have debated over which public administration approach best addresses public issues. In so doing, they draw, to varying degrees, from experiences from past and existing models. The Weberian bureaucracy, though tendentially out of style, is still practiced around the world.With regards to New Public Management (NPM), some authors go as far as saying it 'is dead'[2] while others, instead, argue that while 'on the defensive by now…NPM is very much alive and very much kicking'[3]. NPM remains ingrained in the operationalization of government but under a highly contentious debate *vis-à-vis* the principles of Public Value Management (or *New Public Value*, *Public Value*, or *New Public Service*, to name a few). The commonality among these models is that they each 'reflect different circumstances, different needs and different philosophies about the role of government in society.'[4]

While the compliance-driven Weberian model (or 'old' or 'traditional public administration') focuses primarily on rules and processes, New Public Management model is concerned with efficiencies and business-like effectiveness. Drawing from a number of theories – public choice theory, principal-agent theory, transaction cost economics and competition theory – NPM is regarded more of 'an umbrella term'[5], or more of a kind of 'shopping basket' of public administration reforms[6] than 'a coherent analytical framework'[7]. What connects these definitions, however, are a set of guiding principles widely agreed among scholars[8]. Shifting away from the rigidities of traditional public administration (Weberian model), Hood (1991)[9] argues 'that NPM offers an all-purpose key to better provision of public services' and it does so by relying on principles of (i) hands-on and free-to-manage professional management, (ii) formulation of explicit standards and measures of performance, (iii) greater emphasis on output controls, (iv) disaggregation, (v) competition, (vi) private-sector style of management with greater flexibility in hiring and rewards, and (vii) greater financial discipline and parsimony. In essence, the perceived role of government shifted from a direct service provider to more of a coordinator, a concept Osborn and Gaebler (1992)[10] refer to as 'steering not rowing'.

NPM stands for a 'leaner, and increasingly privatized government, emulating not only the practices but also the values of business'[11]. In line with NPM approach, with small government comes disaggregation – meaning the act of decentralizing government functions to arms' length agencies (a process known as 'agencification'). The irony is that the NPM approach results in an increased number of administrative units and an enlarged scope of government[12]. Furthermore, with agencification, NPM has also created duplication of expenditures and more bureaucratic leadership positions. As a case in point, in the United Kingdom, a '2004 efficiency review conducted for the Treasury concluded that £20 billion of cost savings could be made within four years from a range of measures, including a shift to smarter procurement, carried out by few major procurement centres instead of independently by 270 departments and agencies at the national level'[13].

In view of complexities inherent with agencification, there is also evidence of a government's move towards the recentralization of decentralized functions. One of such efforts was the recentralization of 'major departmental amalgamations at central or federal levels such as the creation of the Department of Homeland Security in the United States…[to address] deficiencies of agency fragmentation highlighted by the 9/11 terrorist [attacks]'[14]. Another is 're-governmentalization' which 'involves the reabsorption into the public sector of activities that had been previously outsourced to the private sector[, *e.g.* the] *de facto* re-nationalization of Railtrack's infrastructure provision functions in the U.K. railways after the company went bankrupt in the summer of 2000'[15].

In sum, 'in the general quest for greater precision and technical certainty,' Gregory (2007)[16] argues, 'NPM has a strong inherent tendency to generate unintended consequences that approximate the obverse of what was intended.' As a result, NPM's 'wave has now largely stalled or been reversed'[17]. This does not mean, however, that NPM is either 'dead'[18] or 'has [entirely] moved into the shadows of history'[19]. In fact, 'NPM practices are extensively institutionalized and will continue just as NPM itself did not displace large elements of previous public administration orthodoxies'[20]. Particularly, 'because of the lag in transferring administrative knowledge and techniques from the developed world to developing regions,…countries in Asia, Africa and Latin America are still in the process of pursuing its remaining elements'[21]. For this reason, Dunleavy *et al.* (2005)[22], go as far as saying that 'in previously laggard areas… [NPM is] apparently flourishing.'

While New Public Management principles (efficiency, economic effectiveness, economizing) remain important and essential, the paradigm has been heavily criticized over the last twenty years, on behalf of 'doing business' in a more inclusive and equitable fashion. This is captured by the Public Value Management paradigm. Public Value Management is particularly concerned with ensuring that whatever procedures and processes are being followed or whatever targets have been met, they all lead to a net benefit to society as whole. We know that just meeting targets not necessarily leads to intended results which, for government, should unqualifiedly be the wellbeing of citizens. PVM's underlying principle is that citizens should actively engage and allowed to engage in decision-making and service delivery, as decisions made affect citizens' lives in a very direct manner.

Public Value Management, however, does not come without criticism either. The *public value* approach raises a number of concerns over definition and measurement. Talbot (2008)[23], for instance, questions whether it is 'possible to have a single public value, in a world of conflicting public values and institutionalized competition between values system', particularly when 'there are conflicting views in society about what might constitute 'the good life' and how we get to it'[24]. Added to the mix, is the notion that 'individuals do not have stable preferences, or even stable ways of thinking about them, but 'flip-flop' between different desires and even ways of thinking about them' simultaneously[25]. Talbot (2008)[26] further contends that even if it would be possible to establish a single concept of public value, it would be quite challenging to measure it.

While Alford and Hughes (2008)[27], recognize that 'what constitutes public value…is much debated…it should be understood that value is not public by virtue of being delivered by the public sector. In fact, it can be produced by government organizations, private firms, nonprofit or voluntary organizations, service users, or various other entities. It is not who *produces* it that makes value public. Rather, it is a matter of who *consumes* it', meaning, "consumed' collectively by the citizenry rather than individually by clients'[28].

That said, in considering approaches, practitioners should not pose the question of 'either/or' (rules and processes *or* efficiency and economic effectiveness *or* citizens participation and value) but rather they should embrace an approach based on inclusion and complementarity, built on a continuum of practices and values. While different circumstances will call for different approaches, it should be possible to sustain a form of government and governance that carries out plans and services based on sound and practical rules (traditional public administration), streamlined processes, business-like practices rather than its values (new public management), designed as efficiency measures to promote effectiveness, all geared towards one single focus – that of the welfare of citizens and their values as citizens themselves see them (public value management), rather than imposed or perceived. This means that, while there is value in old and new public administrations, the citizen rather than the customer should remain sovereign. While co-existence between principles of NPM and values of PVM should be possible, scholars and practitioners' efforts should have been directed all along at focusing on *doing more with better*, meaning with a better governance, rather than of doing *more with less*[29].

While public administration varies from one country to another, public administrators inevitably face similar challenges. Running a government is not easy; it is complex, dynamic, contested, supported, subject to special interests, both demand- and supply-driven, just to name a few. In executing government functions, public administrators unsurprisingly contend with major decision-making questions. While obviously not exhaustive, this book addresses some key issues challenging practitioners. These challenges include questions on what gets included in the policy agenda, questions on policy response to problems through adoption and/or adaptation of exogenous policies, questions on the dangers of displacing policy goals, questions on transferring government activities to specialized agency, questions on decentralizing powers to regional and local governments, questions on combating corruption, and questions on managing public resources.

Chapter Two

Policy Agenda

Agenda-setting is of significant importance in the policy making process. 'At its most basic,' Howlett and Ramesh (2003)[30] sustain 'agenda-setting is about the recognition of a problem on the part of the government' and '[w]hat happens at this early stage has a decisive impact on the entire process and its outcomes.' It is because of this centrality in the policymaking process that government and non-government actors are actively involved. Agenda-setting, as in the case of the remaining stages of the policy making process, is not straight-forward but rather characterized by complexities, convoluted interactions, and constraints, involving institutional structures and a series of influential political actors.

This chapter will address the context within which policy agenda lies and means available for issues to reach the policy agenda, and organizes the analysis into a technical and political setting. The technical setting analysis reviews available models and theories while the political setting analysis reviews how relevant actors and institutional frameworks play a fundamental role in the institutionalization of societal problems.

Policy cycle

Agenda-setting does not exist in a vacuum and it must be viewed within the context of the policy making process. Policy making is complex not only for the reason that it involves many actors but also because any policy is the result of 'a set of interrelated decisions'[31] that cuts across different government agencies and interconnected fields of operation. To complicate matters, trying to understand why a particular decision is made by governments is sometimes obscured by the fact that governments may not necessarily provide a reason, and when they do announce it, it may not necessarily be the actual one[32].

To make sense of the complexities of policy making from an analytical perspective, a number of models were developed that broke down the process into analytically-manageable stages. The first of such models, Lasswell's (1956) model predominantly focuses on the internal decision-making process, thus excluding 'external or environmental influences on government behaviour'[33]. Brewer's (1974) model, instead, expands the analysis 'beyond the confines of the government' and recognizes the indefinite life cycle of a policy, with no clear beginning or end[34]. A more recent five-stage model (agenda-setting, policy formulation, decision-making, policy implementation, and policy evaluation) allows for a more in-depth analysis of actors involved at all stages of the policy making cycle[35]. Its simplistic framework, however, represents also its main disadvantage. Jenkins-Smith and Sabatier (1993)[36] argue that the model can be misinterpreted to suggest that problem-solving is a systematic and linear exercise. Policy making is in reality complex where 'the stages are often compressed or skipped, or followed in an order unlike that specified by the model'[37]. More importantly, the five-stage model 'offers no pointers as to what, or who, drives a policy from one stage to another'[38]. These elements are fundamental in addressing agenda-setting.

Making it to the policy agenda

It is at the stage of the agenda-setting that the list of pressing issues and problems advanced by governments and outside actors is narrowed 'to the set that actually becomes the focus of attention'[39]. The following analysis considers the dynamics involved in agenda-setting within a technical and a political setting.

Technical setting

The technical setting addresses types of agendas, models, and initiation patterns. They provide opportunities and means for policy actors to get involved at the early stage of the policy making process, make their concerns heard and, in so doing, exert necessary pressures to advance their own interests.

The starting point for this analysis lies in what constitutes a problem. Its 'recognition is a socially constructed process...[that]...involves definitions of normalcy and what constitutes an undesirable deviation of the status'[40]. This leads to clashes among policy actors that reveal more about their 'abilities and resources...than...the elegance or purity of the ideas they hold'[41]. Problems can range from issues that reached crisis proportion to issues that raise legitimacy and power concerns, from issues of a human interest to issues that have a wide impact on the people[42]. The viability for issues to make it to the policy agenda is contingent upon opportunities and the promotion of pressing issues by powerful actors involved in the process as well as the constraints and opportunities provided by institutional structures.

Problems reaching agenda-setting stage can be grouped, as per Cobb and Elder (1972)[43], into social problems recognized by the public requiring government action. These problems include societal issues, such as crime and health care and become part of the *systemic* or *informal public agenda*. The shift from systemic to *institutional* or *formal government agenda* occurs when the state recognizes issues raised by the public to be a problem, and it includes other issues the government itself announced it will address that warrant serious consideration. Other problems that make it to the agenda but do not receive much attention are part of the so-called *pseudo-agenda*[44]. The mere recognition of a problem, however, does not necessarily mean that policymakers 'share the same understanding of its causes or ramifications' particularly because they may not necessarily agree on a clear definition of the problem[45].

From a pluralistic perspective, problems are viewed 'as always moving from systemic to institutional agendas'[46] in a stable environment. Recognizing that this is not necessarily the case, Cobb *et al* (1976)[47] developed *models of agenda building*. The *outside initiation model* captures social problems initiated by key social groups external to the formal government structure. Securing the recognition of issues onto the institutional agenda requires political skills and resources to compete against oppositions and other issues. The *mobilization model* addresses issues initiated by decision makers or political leaders and placed on the institutional agenda while 'the public may well be kept in the dark about the policy and its development until its formal announcement.' The public, under this model, is needed for implementing the policy. It is unclear why Cobb and others associated this model to totalitarian regimes, when in fact having to 'require the support of the mass public for implementation' is not necessarily a pressing concern in such political systems. The *inside initiation model* excludes public involvement as government agencies or influential groups do not want issues to be contested by and in public.

Recognizing that all three models presented by Cobb and others could be found within each political regime (democratic, totalitarian, and corporatist, respectively), Kingdon (1984)[48] developed the *policy windows model* also to account for issues that do not necessarily 'originate in the agenda-setting process itself, [but rather]...are developed after an item has moved onto the official agenda'[49]. This model represents another means to view agenda-setting. It is not based on cyclical stages as previous models but rather it recognizes the opportunistic dynamism of policy making.

Partially drawing on the 'garbage-can' principle expounded by March and Olsen (1979)[50] that policy making process is void of rationality and incrementalism, Kingdon's model provides significant opportunities for political actors to gain entrance to agenda-setting, *i.e.* when there may be 'a change of administration, a shift in the partisan or ideological distribution of seats...or a shift in national mood...or a new problem captures the attention of the government officials and those close to them.' The model revolves around the convergence of at least two out of the three independent streams – the *problem stream* (addressing the most pressing problem the public wants something done to change it), the *policy stream* (characterized by the alternatives and proposals championed by interest groups), and the *political stream* (capturing swings in public mood, leadership, interest groups campaign, electoral results). In essence, 'policy windows can be seized' if at least the political stream and the problem stream are linked and placed on the agenda. While March and Olsen (1979) sustain 'that public decisions are often made in too ad-hoc and haphazard fashion'[51] mainly emphasizing the unpredictable nature of the process, Kingdon (1984) sustains that '[w]indows sometimes open with great predictability'[52]. Kingdon's critics argue, however, that his model is yet 'too contingent on unforeseen circumstances, ignoring the fact that in most policy sectors...activities tend to occur in spurts and then congeal for lengthy periods of time' thus failing to recognize the stability of agenda-setting as argued by Cobb[53].

Earlier models did not adequately explain the complexities surrounding agenda-setting. By limiting their efforts to identifying a single cause or factor in trying to explain how problems reach the agenda, earlier models lacked the recognition of multidimensional variables that better characterizes the practice. The *convergence theses*, for instance, sustained that public policies were dependent upon 'the level of economic development of the society in question' rather than other factors like the various actors, cultures, and politics[54]. Moreover, it was widely held that 'high levels of economic development and wealth created similar problems and opportunities, which were dealt with in broadly the same manner in different countries, regardless of the differences in their social or political structures[55]. This one-size-fits-all thesis is by far misleading *vis-à-vis* the realities of public policy making at any level.

Other agenda-setting models include Downs' (1972) *issue-attention cycle*, which characterizes public attention to a problem to be cyclical where it 'suddenly leaps into prominence, remains there for a short time, and then – though still largely unresolved – gradually fades from the center of public attention'[56]. Results of Peters and Hogwood (1985)[57] study of Downs's hypothesis show that 'problems...receive a higher level of attention after rather than before the peak.' Moreover, they identify two additional cycles – one that deals with external events and one that deals with events initiated by the political leadership, both mediated by the public with a good possibility that neither would fade away.

Political setting

As we have seen from the above models, the evolution of analytical study led to the recognition that arenas of agenda-setting and policy making as a whole are dynamic, contentious, and converging points for powerful interests, influences, and divergence. Securing recognition of an issue onto the institutional agenda is far from being solely technical. Access is unequal and the process is intrinsically political. To identify who decides, why, and in whose interests decisions are made, one is to address the extent to which power is exercised by institutions and political actors, including networks.

Contrary to the pluralists view, Schattschneider (1960) argues that governments are not at all neutral but powerful actors able 'to constrain and filter out conflict before it start...[and where]...powerful political elites...manage and manipulate the political process to their own ends'[58]. This argument is supported by Easton (1965) model of agenda control that recognizes all actors as *gatekeepers* whose function is 'to exclude from the system excessive, or unacceptable, demands'[59]. Bachrach and Baratz (1970)[60] further argue that bias exists on the part of systems towards key groups, including the public. They contend that a 'second face of power' exists that captures 'the crucial role non-decisions...play in setting the policy agenda'. This means that 'demands for change...can be suffocated before they are even voiced.' This theory was developed to make sense of global economic developments in the late 1960s at a time when the state was highly pressured, among others, by multinational corporations' significant economic and political power.

It is important to recognize that the way a problem is defined is conditioned by the values institutional frameworks uphold[61]. In explaining the power interaction among all entities, one is to consider the overall role that institutional frameworks play in policy making.

Institutions matter as they set the tone for political interactions by dictating the 'rules of the game'[62]. These rules influence people's behaviour. It is argued that it is precisely within the context of institutional frameworks that political actors define their role in pursuit of specific self-interests[63]. For instance, Swank (2002)[64] argues that institutions, whether social corporatist or pluralist, inclusive or exclusive electoral systems, with dispersed or concentrated power distribution, 'provide opportunities for resistance to unwanted change; influence the relative power of groups; promote values…important to welfare.' Moreover, '[p]re-existing institutional frameworks [meaning old policies]…often allocate resources to some options rather than others, affecting the relationship between different policy strategies and privileging some actors over others'[65].

Immergut (1992)[66] claims that while it is difficult to sustain the argument that institutions can predict outcomes, it is possible to use an analysis of the institutional structure 'to predict the ways in which these policy conflicts will be played out.' By analysing the opportunities or *veto points* (in the executive, parliament, or electoral process, respectively) available in Sweden, France, and Switzerland granted by constitutional rules and electoral results, Immergut (1992) emphasizes the direct influence institutional structures have on the outcome of decision-making. In the process, the analysis also supports the argument advanced by Pierson (1995)[67], who argues that the fragmentation of political systems such as federalism creates veto opportunities and influences interests. The federal constitution, in fact, fosters the permanency of regional distribution of resources onto the agenda. But in so doing, Pierson

(1995)[68] argues that the regional dimension constitutes a 'significant political cleavage (between regions)...in key political debates' that are inexistent in unitary states.

'[T]he mode of agenda-setting', it is argued by Kingdon (1984) and Baumgarten and Jones (1991)[69], 'is determined by the nature of public support for the issue and by the nature of the initiating actor(s).' In this regard, further to institutional structures, analysis of policy networks and their interactions in the political arena constitute another major influential approach to explain policy agenda-setting. Acting 'as filters that shape the ways in which specific policy sectors respond to common pressures', policy networks 'deter radical change and foster incremental change' and are 'most powerful when combined with others explanation of change'[70]. Also, policy networks aliment the intertwined dependency surrounding public policy making. While policy networks represent the interests of political players, policy network analysis concedes that interactions between them are not necessarily one-sided. In fact, the analysis 'recognizes that government actors need to establish relationships with interest groups to obtain information, support and legitimacy for decision-making'[71]. Moreover, governments do 'play a key role in the formation of policy networks,...often determining what type of interest gains access'[72]. These recognitions support the relational dialectical approach expounded by Marsh and Smith (2000)[73], which departs from previous policy network models. They argue, in fact, that Dowding's rational choice approach, McPherson and Raab's anthropological approach, Laumann and Knobe's formal policy network, and Marsh and Rhode's structural approach 'all fail to recognize that any attempt to use policy networks as an explanatory variable involves three dialectical relationships that exists between structure and agency; network and context; and network and outcome'[74]. These elements are important as networks are themselves political structures with endogenous cultures and rules that can constrain or foster opportunities for their own agents' behaviour *vis-à-vis* networks' objective to exert pressure on behalf of a specific issue[75]. Furthermore, Marsh and Smith (2000)[76] argue that other analyses, such as that of Marsh and Rhodes (1992), 'fail to examine another important constraint on networks: other networks.' This omission undermines the already existent complexities surrounding networks' operations.

Policy networks exist 'to promote and protect their interests through involvement in policy making and co-operation in policy implementation'[77]. More specifically, Marsh and Rhodes (1992)[78] sustain 'that policy networks exist to restrict access to the policy-making process [and]...to promote stability and continuity' thus constituting a significant constant variable in influencing what gets considered or not in the institutional agenda. Baumgarten and Jones (1991)[79] further argue that '[t]he key element in the process of agenda-setting,... revolves around...the ability to [gain] control [of] the interpretation of a problem and thus the manner in which it is conceived and discussed.' This argument leads to the possible adoption of two strategies – one based on 'encouraging the public to call upon the government to resolve [the problem]', the other by altering the image of the problem by those who 'do not like the problems being developed or discussed by the government' through expanding or contracting the membership of the institutional arrangements within which they operate[80].

In essence, 'policy networks foster incremental changes, thereby favouring the *status quo* or the existing balance of interests[81]. Nonetheless, Howlett and Ramesh (2003)[82] sustain that 'decisions by governments to retain the status quo are just as much policy as are decisions to alter it.' Policy networks analysis does not come without its critics, however. Dowding (1995)[83], for instance, argues that the analysis 'lacks explanatory power' as it 'fails to produce fundamental theories of the policy process' with no regard to the actual structure or 'characteristics of components within the networks.'

Concluding remarks

The purpose of this review was not to prescribe specific and preparatory chronological steps for policy actors and institutional structures to influence policy agenda-setting, particularly because the politicking of securing an issue onto the policy agenda highlights the complexities and the non-linearity of policy making. The aim, instead, was to recognize the centrality of agenda-setting in the political process, analyse the available tools (models and theories) used to make sense of the process, while considering the influential role institutional frameworks and policy networks play in public policy making discourse. While Lundquist (1987)[84] sustains 'that both actors and institutions play a crucial role in the policy process', Hudson and Lowe (2004)[85] recognize there is 'no magic-wand solution that answers all the questions about how and why policy enters (or does not enter) the agenda.' One needs, therefore, to look beyond the dictum of a single model or theory and encompass, instead, various approaches to make sense of the complexities inherent to policy agenda and the political process as whole. *In fine*, it is precisely because of the role agenda-setting plays in the political process and its centrality 'to virtually all concepts of power and influence that we are required to search for new and better methods to improve our understanding'[86].

Policy Transfer

Policy transfer is 'about the transposition of policies and/or practices already in operation in one jurisdiction to another'[87] and concerns both voluntary and coerced transfers. Most policy transfers occur across developed countries, from developed to developing, and within countries. A glimpse of potential South-North transfer can be associated to the Asian financial market where, up to '1997 many government leaders in the Western world were talking about learning from the so-called Asian 'miracle''[88]. Nonetheless, owing to the financial crisis, high profile Asian countries 'fell out of favour' and no longer could 'Asian leaders...preach to the West about the 'Asian Way' or the requirement to 'look East''[89]. Surprisingly, in an age where information can be at our finger tips, the seemingly lack of documented evidence of an inverse dialectical influence – from developing to developed countries – begs the question: Do developing countries really have nothing to teach the developed world? And if they do, as it is inconceivable it could be otherwise, why is there limited, if at all, information on South-North transfer? This initial finding suggests further research in needed.

Organized along the following lines, this chapter will consider principles of policy transfer, opportunities as well as conceptual, empirical, and practical limitations. The chapter argues that opportunities in one case can represent limitations under different circumstances.

Principles

While 'many problems facing a government have counterparts elsewhere'[90], 'it does not assume that there must be, or even can be, a common response' nor that 'finding a programme that has brought political satisfaction elsewhere guarantee[s] that it can be transferred effectively'[91]. In spite of this, '[t]hose concerned about improving the quality and/or rationality of decision-making would agree that engaging in a search process of policies and practices in other countries or jurisdictions is more comprehensive and thorough than a limited exercise of adjusting policy heuristics'[92]. Gonzalez (2007)[93] cautions, however, about rushing into policy transfer and argues for 'the urgent need to endow local policy makers the capacity to analyse their own situation and tailor policy to fit domestic context, rather than simply apply standard models.'

As the more recognized definition of policy transfer, Dolowitz and Marsh (1996)[94] define it as 'a process in which knowledge about policies, administrative arrangements, institutions etc. in one time and/or place is used in the development of policies, administrative arrangements and institutions in another time and/or place.' Their characterization stands as a chapeau definition that encompasses also studies on lesson-drawing, policy convergence, and policy diffusion. Two key points stand out from their definition. 'Knowledge' denotes a voluntaristic effort by governments to learn about other policies and apply them domestically. The term 'used', on the other hand, does not exclude the possibility of a coerced application of policies. At the end of Dolowitz and Marsh (2000)[95] *policy transfer continuum*, voluntarily acquiring knowledge would be an exercise onto itself unless 'lesson-drawing seeks to use knowledge from other times and places to improve current programmes', while also determining its feasibility of transfer into local settings[96]. Success already encountered elsewhere provides the adopting country with legitimacy 'therefore, boost[ing] the rationality of the policy-making process, allowing decision makers to consider a wide range of policy options and a broader base of evidence about their impact'[97].

At the opposite end of the model are coercive transfers, mostly involving supranational organizations, for example, the European Union, the International Monetary Fund (IMF), and the World Bank[98]. The latter two organizations, 'bring with them preconceived ideas, the principles on which policy should operate, and often tie assistance in meeting social problems to policy reforms'[99]. This imposition is particularly evident concerning 'those [less powerful nations] in urgent need of aid or additional foreign investment...[where] these transnational institutions can almost dictate the nature of the policy change'[100]. Conditionality imposed by international lending institutions on macroeconomic frameworks cause destructive consequences to developing countries, particularly concerning social sectors[101]. For instance, en face the ravages of HIV/AIDS, Malawi found itself grossly short of total number of nurses (two thirds short) and doctors (90 percent short) required[102]. Despite this critical deficiency in human capacity, Malawi was not 'allowed to hire more staff and pay better salaries, because it would breach the macroeconomic' policies imposed by the IMF[103]. Conditionality has not spared developed countries either. In the 1970s, for example, the IMF imposed conditions, which included public spending reductions and inflation control measures, to a loan the United Kingdom had sought to face 'a persistent and significant weakness of the pound...and a related balance of payments problem'[104].

Opportunities and limitations

To avoid dispersiveness, this section addresses only a few factors that contribute and/or limit policy transfer. It highlights opportunities and limitations associated with globalization, epistemic communities, and affinities. The section also addresses conceptual and empirical limitations. The aim is to provide, to the extent possible, evidence that at least some factors associated with policy transfer can facilitate in one case and frustrate the transposition of policies in another.

Alternative ways to address domestic problems are sought by policymakers when gaps between aspiration and achievement exist[105]. While doing nothing about the problem constitutes a policy decision and an option, dissatisfaction with the *status quo* can create opportunities to search for solutions abroad or within country. A number of conditions may lead to dissatisfaction. For Stone (1999)[106], 'crisis and political conflict, the absence of a scientific consensus or a lack of information,… new problems and policy disaster potentially induce…policy makers to look at experiments elsewhere that have been developed in response to similar conditions of uncertainty.' While crisis and uncertainty can be preconditions which stimulate change[107], Gonzalez (2007)[108] argues policy transfer 'can be the source of uncertainty and instability, if the innovation brought in from aboard is inappropriate, or coercively adapted.'

To mention a few examples when policy transfer might take place, 'regime transformation (such as the breakdown of the Soviet Union) creates opportunity for transfer in the construction of new constitutions, creation of market system of exchange or taxation codes'[109]. The HIV/AID pandemic, as well, 'prompted health experts, NGOs and officials to look at practices elsewhere as guides of action on *inter alia*, 'safe sex' advertising, immigration policies, medical research funding and community care'[110]. For Rose (1991)[111] shifts in political values are reflections of 'dissatisfaction with programmes that formerly had operated by routine…for example, the series of anti-poverty programmes that constituted the 1960s American War on Poverty was not much a response to increased poverty as it was a consequence of a shift in values that produced a demand to 'do something' about poverty.' The preceding examples of opportunities can be framed within Kingdon's (1984)[112] *policy windows model* which provides a significant political opening to gain entrance to policy decision-making through what he defines problem, policy, and political streams.

Contemporary world is more than ever 'connected in ways that were imaginable even a few decades ago' where access to and speed of information exchanges and rapid transportation across great distances induce us 'to rethink our understanding of the nature of 'society' with its relatively fixed social structures and geographical boundaries'[113]. As a result of globalization, countries strive to 'maximise the[ir] ability... to keep pace with change' by restructuring, adopting, and adapting new ways of doing business based on devolved fragmented structures, public-private partnerships, and new layers of governance, rather than centralized governments and top-down hierarchies[114]. Global exposure and pressures, therefore, provide policymakers opportunities to search for alternatives elsewhere in order not to lose ground and in response to problems highlighted by similar conditions elsewhere. The transposition of policies further 'facilitates processes of globalization...through the creation of further opportunity structures, such as European Union (EU) economic development programmes'[115]. Globalization, as per Cerny (1992)[116], transforms 'the nation-state into a competition state.'This 'transformation...lies at the heart of political globalization'[117]. It is not surprising, however, that counter-argument to globalization would come from less advantaged countries, for their inability to transform themselves into a 'competitive state' for lack of resources and expertise. Poor countries are not well positioned to obtain optimal benefit from this new environment because their negotiating power is rendered unfavorable 'by their weak productive position and export of primary goods, low technology, poor financial strength, unstable economy, poor infrastructure facilities, insecurity and instability in governance'[118].

A natural by-product of globalization is the development of best practices practically on all subject matters. The example that follows highlights limitations to the transposition of best practices, which are normally well advertised through global channels of communications. Best practices could be undermined by the capacity and receptivity by the importer country. Srivastana (2004)[119], in fact, cautions about an '[i]nstitutional reform that ignores the role of local variation...[as it would result in being] at best inadequate, and at worse harmful.' In essence, policy transfer generally works best when consideration is given to the *adaptation* of best practices into a domestic best fit. The case of the Philippines' planning and budgeting reform highlights limitations of transferring best practices, as well as disparate organizational and political structures, capacities, and receptivity to policy and practices transferred. To respond to Philippines' problems with public expenditure management, Australia and the Philippines co-established a programme focused on fiscal reform based on a medium-term expenditure framework and the devolution to programme agencies of financial and management decision-making[120]. The transfer involved the transposition of practices that were 'supposed to complement indigenous knowledge with up-to-date systems that have worked effectively in other countries'[121]. The establishment of a medium-term budget framework required 'interdepartmental coordination...as a way to build support, and avoid inconsistencies and bottlenecks in the implementation process'[122]. Despite the objective, owing to 'the different stages of their own reform' participating oversight government agencies gave way to 'reform silos'[123] which were further exacerbated by disagreement 'on coordination, harmonisation and reorganisation'[124]. Additional constraints resulted from the 'markedly [organizational differences] between the agencies', their 'low absorptive capacity...to participate in the reform activities... [and their] resistance to reforms in light of the instability, perceived or otherwise, on their working conditions'[125]. The transfer was compromised by lack of participation by Congress which 'should have been encouraged to sign up for the reform effort early on'[126]. The case highlights that 'policies, no matter how attractive, cannot be grafted on markedly different blueprints of state-society relations than those in which they evolved'[127]. In this case, the organizational structures of the two countries continue to be 'as different as apples and oranges'[128]. While Australia operates a federal government, the Philippines are a unitary state with a strong central government. Furthermore, '[m]edium-term budget frameworks are administratively and politically demanding, and have been implemented mainly in advanced economies'[129]. The Philippines lacks these capacities. With such dissimilarity, leading to the inevitable alteration of Australia's model down to a best fit, it would have been more adequate for the Philippines to borrow from smaller and similarly-situated countries, taking advantage also of epistemology communities across those countries[130].

Epistemic communities (think tanks, policy transfer network) play a central role in the dissemination of ideas and diffusion of knowledge. 'Policy transfer networks are an action-oriented phenomenon set up with the specific intention of engineering policy change'[131]. Their role is even more so emphasized and sought when decision-makers rely on them for new ideas and for 'develop[ing] the…political and knowledge resources necessary to satisfy successful policy development'[132]. Stone (2000)[133] recognizes how 'market-liberal think tanks in Britain, Australia, and the USA and elsewhere have been important in spreading consensual knowledge and technical information about privatization'. In the UK, for example, '[t]he Institute of Economic Affairs (IEA) was important in developing the intellectual case for privatization, deregulation and the unfettered operation of market forces…[just as] the Centre for Policy Studies (CPS) played a role in privatization debates'[134]. On the other hand, epistemic communities can limit policy transfer. The independence of epistemic communities, in fact, as argued by Gray (1978)[135], may be undermined when 'it is likely that funding criteria influences their agenda and sometimes even their finding.' There are also other circumstances where internationally accepted regimes and their diffusion provoke local resentment. Youde (2005)[136], for example, makes reference to the establishment of 'counter-epistemic communities' in South Africa against international AIDS control regimes that were seemingly successful elsewhere across the globe. South Africa does not share the same 'common knowledge, causal belief, and meanings' of HIV/AIDS[137]. This is based on previous negative experiences with public health in Africa, including the blaming of Africa for the disease' which was seen 'as symptomatic of continued Western racism'[138].

Though not limited to, Pierson (2003)[139] argues that '[s]imilarities of culture, public services, legal practice and above all language have long been seen to tie Anglophone politics into a distinctive 'family of nations'.' Peck and Theodore (2001)[140] further argue that '[p]olicy transfers are likely to be facilitated in institutions where there is alignment of political aspiration and strategies', as well. They argue that the United States and the United Kingdom, for example, 'have embraced a common analysis of the 'welfare problem', facilitated the adoption of overlapping policy discourses, and culminating in the deployment of mutually referential policy measures'[141]. Aside from the perception of the Thatcher government of the success, at least in part, of the US Child Support Enforcement System, the establishment of a British Child Support Agency, for instance, was also based on a similar ideological perspective shared with the Regan administration in the 1990s[142]. Another example of political affinities is Blair's Progressive Governance Summit among centre-left leaders of thirteen other nations that purposely gathered 'to increase the activities of [their existing] network and widen its reach in order to exchange progressive ideas' where each country 'would make particular efforts to draw on the policy experiences of other countries in the network'[143]. On the other hand, political and ideological divergences can limit policy transfer. The ideological divide between the American and Soviet blocks during the Cold War, as a poignant example, was by definition not conducive to policy transfer. When ideologies are so divergent among nations, rather than importation of policies, we can actually witness the passing of policies specifically targeted to repudiate the value system of the contrasting ideologies. Clear examples may come, *inter alia*, in the form of economic sanctions against communist Cuba and the rest of the communist block as well as against Apartheid in South Africa.

While some practical limitations were highlighted above, there are other fundamental limitations of policy transfer that concern concept and empiricism. Conceptually, Dolowitz and Marsh's (1996) model is 'a general framework of heterogeneous concepts including policy diffusion, policy convergence, policy learning and lesson drawing'[144]. While they 'have provided an extremely useful framework', Evans and Davies (1999)[145] point out, 'it is at best a heuristic model…[that lacks the ability] to determine with precision the phenomenon it is trying to explain.' In a similar vein, James and Lodge (2003)[146]argue that Dolowitz and Marsh's (1996, 2000) model 'obscures' 'into a single dimension of difference' dimensions of perfect and bounded rationality. While Dolowitz and Marsh (2000)[147] contend that the model 'can be used by researchers to frame their empirical work' and that, by recognizing 'many cases of transfer involve both voluntary and coercive elements', James and Lodge (2003)[148] argue that in so doing, they achieve a different effect whereby the 'framework obscures the potential range of different explanation of the policy-making processes', instead.

Finally, empirical limitations concern the demonstrability that policy transfer did actually take place. Global connectivity, where local issues gain a broader audience, has 'made it easier and faster for policy-makers to communicate with each other, [and for this reason] the occurrences of policy transfer have increased'[149]. In response, however, James and Lodge (2003)[150] argue, as also sustained by Evans and Davies (1999)[151], that without 'clear measures of transfer...[it would be difficult] to assess whether the amount of knowledge of other places utilised in policy-making has over time increased, decreased, remained the same or changed in some other way.' Dolowitz, Greenwold, and Marsh (1999)[152] further argue that quantifying the extent of voluntary transfers is not possible, particularly because '[g]overnments do not provide convenient lists of what they borrowed, or from where they borrow.' In order to determine whether transfer occurred, one needs 'to establish that [importers]...were searching for a policy, that [they] visited [exporters] to examine a policy/electoral strategy, and that key elements of this were incorporated into [the importer's] practice and/or legislation.' The criteria is further developed by Bennett (1997)[153] who sustains that to 'convincingly make the case that cross-national policy learning has had a determining influence on policy change', the following criteria need to be met: 'idiosyncratic domestic factors are not independently responsible for the policy adoption..., the adoption is not the result of similar modernising forces having the same, but separate effects in different states..., that policy makers are aware of the policy adoptions elsewhere...,[and finally] that oversee evidence was utilized within domestic policy debates'[154].

Concluding remarks

We have seen that divergent intentionality characterizes the principles of policy transfer. On the one hand, we have the voluntary importation of innovatory policies from one context to another 'in the belief...[policies] will be similarly successful' in a different context[155]. On the other, we have the coerced importation of policies imposed by international and supranational organizations that shape domestic policies. In either scenario, the only constant remains the voluntaristic exportation on the part of outside actors.

From a voluntaristic perspective, while policy transfer may provide policymakers a 'quick fix' *en face* 'increasingly complex and quickly changing policy environment'[156], caution should be exercised towards adopting ready-made best practices without prior adapting them to an idiosyncratic domestic best fit, instead.

What should also stand out, however, from the review is the apparent lack of 'focused reference to South-North traffic'[157] of policy transfers. '[B]y failing to acknowledge that policy entrepreneurs in the North may have something to learn from successful programmes already underway in the South,' argues Nedley (2004)[158], 'policy transfer search activity is wholly irrational...[T]he exclusion by Northern policy-makers of developing country experience suggests an unhealthy inability or unwillingness to access what 'the-other-half' knows. This approach inhibits the opportunity for genuine global dialogue and, in turn, confines both policy learning and transfer.' This apparent literary shortage should encourage further research.

Chapter Four

Goal Displacement

'Goal displacement' is a term associated with Merton (1940)[159] that captures a phenomenon by which the operational focus on the *means* overtakes the organizational strategic focus on the *ends*, which the means were originally supposed to support in the first place. Recognized as one of the drawbacks of bureaucratic structures, Merton narrowly places the focus of this transformation primarily on the rigid and blind adherence to rules as 'absolutes…rather than strictly utilitarian'[160]. The chapter will show, however, that goals displacement is not limited to the organizational sanctification of rules as the *raison d'etre* but rather it expands also to include peripheral objectives and performance targets. As goal displacement is a symptom of a natural condition of human nature – self-preservation, – it would be hard not to recognize its inevitable occurrence and exclude its applicability also to new normative organizations.

While not exhaustive, at least three types of manifestations can be identified concerning goal displacement. Their focus concerns rules, regulations, and procedures, as well as performance targets and peripheral objectives.

Losing sight of its primary purpose, an organization can easily make 'conformity with prescribed patterns of actions…[meaning rules and] regulations, whatever the situation,…an immediate value in the life-organization of the bureaucrat'[161]. Merton (1940)[162] identifies the 'bureaucratic virtuoso, who never forgets a single rule binding his action and hence is unable to assist many of his clients' as the natural and immediate by-product of goal displacement.

It would be inconceivable to think that the original purpose of any public organization would be to meet targets rather than a more purposeful objective, such as to improve the lives of the citizenry. When organizations are held accountable for meeting targets, however, as often is the case, the focus can inevitably shift from the main objective. In so doing and despite meeting the targets, the mere hitting does not guarantee the attainment of the goals.

Goal displacement also entails revising the course of the original organizational goals by replacing or superseding them with secondary ones. This may be the result also of the realization that goal-setting did not fully take into account implementation projections, meaning organizational capacities and financial resources to carry out the necessary activities aimed at achieving the goals.

Causes, consequences, and inevitability

Practically anything can trigger goal displacement. It should be recognized, however, that at least three categories may exist – one where the phenomenon is generated by the principle of self-preservation in response to internal and external factors; another which is caused by the 'bureaucratic virtuoso' whose concern is merely to follow rules, regardless; another where the focus on rules is a means to maintain tight control *vis-à-vis* a threat to the survival of the organization. The chapter addresses the former category.

Goals displacement may be caused, *inter alia*, by pressures from 'modern conditions of high change and turbulence'[163], the vagueness of the objective, dominance of a group, leadership ideology changes, mismatch between the goal-setting process and the realities of organizational constraints[164], increased accountability, and reward systems[165].

As argued by Warner and Havens (1968)[166], '[g]oal displacement is minimal where goals are tangible.' Intangible goals concern those that are difficult to measure, *e.g.* 'helping people become better citizens, developing greater community integration or stronger community spirit, developing attitudes and skills of cooperation'[167]. This is why governments find it much easier to measure performance at the output rather than at the outcome level. The efforts required with measuring the attainment of intangible goals leads to problems that follow the principle of 'what gets measured gets done'[168]. Owing to the inherent complexities of 'public policy realm', 'social interventions are particularly vulnerable to lack of attention to what is really important because it is difficult to measure'[169]. In the end '[w]hat gets measured, or even measurable, often bears little resemblance to what is relevant'[170]. Focusing on performance measures based on irrelevant, inaccurate or unreliable data leads to meeting criteria that bears little resemblance to the programme's *raison d'etre*…[This] is called 'perverse incentives'[171].

Goal displacement is bound when the process of organizational goal-setting is divorced from the capacity analysis demanded by the implementation phase[172]. The asymmetry between the two phases is not uncommon. With the aim of revitalizing the Southside neighborhood in Racine, Michigan, for instance, a committee was established to represent neighborhood interests. For the most part, especially for the first year, the committee 'devoted most of its efforts to developing [, through funding applications to federal agencies,] resources necessary to ensure its continued existence and the implementation of its programs'[173]. Lack of funding from federal agencies resulted in a 'substantial shortfall in the number rehabilitated units from the scale originally planned'[174]. As the committee grew, it was reorganized as a business with greater focus on business development rather than housing, with financial backing from local business corporation rather than federal agencies[175]. Alexander (1976) categorizes the unfolding of the genesis and development of the neighborhood committee as a case of 'resource oriented' goal displacement aimed at survival[176]. While the priorities were rearranged, the shift was further 'accentuated by the emergence of a distinct of administrators and policy makers' more oriented towards business[177]. This case highlights the inevitable consequences of tallying up the bill without the host, meaning the lack of due consideration for securing adequate resources during the implementation in line with the goal setting phase. Simply put, '[t]here is no point in having good ideas if they cannot be carried out....Implementation must not be conceived as a process that takes place after, and independent of, the design of policy'[178].

Similarly, goal displacement by shift of peripheral goals in the case of an adult day care center in the United States can also be attributed to asymmetries between plans and resources. While CADC 'was ostensibly founded to care for and improve the lives of elders with dementia, the center instead focused on providing respite for family caregivers who depended on the center for relief from care-giving'[179]. Providing respite constituted the second formal aim of the center, the third being delaying permanent institutionalization[180]. Providing respite to the caregivers required no additional costs. On the other hand, aiming 'to improve the lives of the elderly...would have required a great of unavailable resources'[181]. Maintaining adequate funding had been a constant struggle for CADC. The center was heavily reliant on in-kind contributions, volunteers, subsidies, and grants as it could not meet its costs solely on public funding and private payments[182]. Owing to organizational and financial constraints, CADC found itself organizing its work around a secondary goal (respite) and around the means (caregivers) through which, *inter alia*, the center had hoped to improve the lives of the patients (CADC original goal and primary clients). Improving the lives of its patients was therefore not directly addressed for lack of resources, both in terms of staffing and financial feasibility.

Pressures, both internal and external, may lead an organization to detract from its originally-intended course and focus, instead, on survival. When organizational survival is on the line, it is not uncommon to divert its original goal towards others that yield better chances of staying afloat and of sustainability. The original goal of the United Nations

Food and Agriculture Organisation (FAO), for instance, is to feed the world's population[183]. In light of the reality that agriculture today is 'controlled…by big companies to sell the inputs and big companies… that buy the produce, process and market it', the FAO has found itself at the mercy of these big companies and the funding governments who have an intimate interests 'in selling the inputs that their industries produce, such as fertilizers and pesticides, and helping their engineering companies build dams and selling turbines for them. This means that the FAO is condemned to promoting high-input agriculture, which cannot feed the world'[184]. The way agriculture is run worldwide 'works against the FAO's aims' in the sense that (i) farmers cannot afford the costs and are forced out of business, and (ii) owing to the interests requirements on the loans, farmers are forced to export what they produce leaving very little to feed local people[185].

The pressures of a reward systems, Kerr (1975)[186] argues, tend to cause goal displacement whereby 'behaviors which are awarded are those which the rewarder is trying to *discourage*, while the behaviour he desires is not being awarded at all.' In the case of orphanages, for instance, Kerr argues that ideally the objective is 'placing as many children as possible in good homes. However, often [they] surround themselves with so many rules concerning adoption that is nearly impossible to pry a child out of the place.'[187] When viewed in terms of the criteria for receiving funding (*i.e.*number of children enrolled) and the director's prestige (based on organizational size and total number of children under the director's care), 'it becomes rational for them to make it difficult for children to be adopted'[188]. On the other hand, goal displacement is also likely to occur if the reward system would be based on number of placements[189]. This is also evident in rewarding rehabilitation centers 'for the number of individuals placed in any position for 60 days or more', covering particularly individuals with relative skills while ignoring individuals with lesser skills and therefore harder to place[190].

Meeting performance targets places pressures onto organizations, potentially causing them to regroup and alter their course. As argued by Walker (2009)[191], while the goal of the American education system is to properly educate all students, this primary objective is traded off by an alternative goal of testing a subset of students (meaning excluding groups of children) with the sole scope to increase scores on standardized tests that will make the district look favorably on performance measures (meaning, better scores = more funding, better reputation). Goal displacement occurs when there are systematic and rigid pressures to perform well. '[T]he American educational system has become engulfed in high-stakes testing' which can lead to students 'being held back a year, or being prevented from graduating'[192], schools not receiving funding, tarnished reputation, teachers not receiving salary raises, and 'narrow[ing] the academic curriculum to meet the needs of the tests'[193]. 'The No Child Left Behind Act introduced one of the most rigorous accountability systems for education in United States history...creating an incentive system based on allocation of resources'[194] by which funds can be withheld among many other threats. Organizational cheating will inevitably occur. By cheating, it is intended the intentional 'manipulat[ion of] output levels to portray their work in the best light'[195]. Cheating can range from purposely teaching to take tests, actual erasing and manipulating students' standardized scores, excluding low performing students from taking the test either by placing them in special education courses or convincing them not to show up on the test date[196]. Organizational cheating involving students may also be what Bohte and Meier (2000)[197] classify as cutting corners to enhance their performance rating by 'graduat[ing] illiterate students simply to push their graduation rates higher.' The end result is, to the detriment of the students, the adherence to the displaced objective (achieving targets) rather than the benevolent objective that all students should get out of school educated,–a groundbreaking and *nouvelle idée*, perhaps.

While 'scarce institutional resources and difficult task demands are major factors that prompt bureaucrats to rely on a strategy of cheating[198], organizational cheating is more 'likely to occur in organizations where the day-to-day activities of bureaucrats are not heavily monitored, *i.e.* highly decentralized bureaucracies'[199]. 'The lack of continuous and direct monitoring gives street-level bureaucrats a great deal of discretion in how they implement policies. Knowing they must produce a certain level of outputs, street-level bureaucrats may see a lack of constant monitoring from supervisors as an opportunity to cheat in hopes of maximizing program outputs'[200].

As we have seen, displacing organizational goals down to meeting performance targets creates an expectation of reward and survival. Goal displacement in the cases above deals with reprioritization of goals during the implementation phase as an 'afterthought', as a readjustment of organizational inceptive goals. What happens, though, when the original design is flawed and meeting targets does not meet goals? Leeuw[201] defines this phenomenon as 'performance paradox'. Stribu (2008)[202] applies this paradox to the aimed achievement of the *United Nations Millennium Development Goals (MDGs)*. The MDGs are a global action plan to achieve priority goals by the target date of 2015 against poverty, hunger and disease, women's and children health, gender equality, education, sustainable development and global partnerships[203]. Stribu (2008)[204] recognizes that '[w]hile being necessary goals, the MDGs are not *sufficient* to achieve socially equitable, inclusive and just development [if]...each goal [is pursued] in isolation of the others, without understanding and exploring the linkages between them, and the synergies in outcomes that they can generate,...[this shortfall] risks overlooking crucial opportunities for results. Identifying and building on visible and invisible policy linkages can help un-block and strengthen the potential of the MDGs'. A holistic approach can potentially unravel the complexity of MDGs achievement, whereby reducing poverty and hunger, for instance, should be based on focusing on poverty and inequality rather than on poverty alone[205]. Sundaram (2007)[206] argues, in fact, that 'inequality, in both income and wealth, has been increasing over the last several decades..., and acting as a counter force to poverty reduction'. That is the reason why addressing various angles of societal problems would potentially reap better chances for the successful attainment on the goals. Furthermore, Elson (2004)[207] posits that applying the 'international one-dollar-a-day definition and measurement of poverty...uniformly across the board,

[will] result...in a situation where even if millions are alleviated from poverty, their situation will barely improve if living costs are higher than the international poverty line assumes.' Stribu (2008)[208] also identifies 'limitations in relation to gender equality and empowerment, which is measured by sex parity in primary education. It distracts attention from important issues of equality of sexual and reproductive rights relating to deep structural factors and of power relations, which are at the root of the perpetration of gender inequality and oppression.'

Goal displacement is inevitable. It is inevitable in bureaucratic organizations just as in new normative organizations and it takes place at all levels. The intimate interplay between needing to be flexible *vis-à-vis* internal and external demands coupled with the drive to survive inevitably leads to a reactive or proactive organizational distraction from its originally intended goal. While it may not be a sure occurrence in all organizations and under all circumstances, the inevitable tendency of its occurrence should be recognized because of its underlying principle – that of *self-preservation*.

As a case in point, Merton (1940)[209] argues that bureaucratic functionaries, while able to minimize in-group aggression because of their shared interests, they also have the potential 'to defend their entrenched interests rather than to assist their clientele and elected higher officials.' Defending entrenched interests is not reserved to bureaucratic organizations alone. It takes place in our personal lives and it certainly takes place in new normative organizations, where integrative teamwork is highly emphasized. Child (2005)[210] argues, for instance, that while top management teams 'are formed to coordinate policy formulation and implementation across the different units of the organization...[they] do not always achieve integration desired because of the high level of individualism that characterizes many senior managers'. Coordinators of teams may also astray in goal displacement and outlive their originally-intended usefulness when they engage in 'empire-building..., start to oppose attempts at simpler forms of direct integration that appear to bypass them..., attempt to monopolize coordination and block more innovative solutions'[211]. Furthermore, in addressing output control strategy, Child (2005)[212] highlights an inherent danger that threatens the principle upon which new normative organizations are founded – that of achieving results. Performance is potentially threatened by 'the autonomy given to working groups or teams, which output control encourages, [and this] can stand in the way of introducing technological advances that require a more integrated process combining tasks previously performed separately by the groups'[213].

Concluding remarks

In the public sector, the rationale for government interventions is to produce benefits, or results, for its citizens[214]. Nonetheless, owing to pressures for survival, emphasis is endemically placed on the process, on rules, on distorting performance data in order to meet targets. In so doing, organizations lose sight of the originally intended outcome and lose focus on what is necessary to get the job done to achieve that outcome or at least make a positive change to ameliorate the situation of the citizenry that required attention in the first place.

Goal displacement discourse revolves around the divergence from an organization's founding purpose. The chapter addressed causes like the vagueness of the objective, dominance of a group, mismatch between the goal-setting process, realities of organizational constraints and reward systems and applied the aforementioned to cases in the public sector. The high volatility of external conditions, *inter alia*, drives organizations to adapt to new demands. In order to adapt, something has to give. While lesser objectives become the priority and easier targets and the over-reliance on rules and processes become the new organizational focus, the underlying objective of goal displacement boils down to self-preservation.

michael anthony

tarallo

Chapter Five

Agencification

Agencification 'is a major trend in the management of public services, based on the idea that the policy arms of government can be separated from the executive or implementation arms'[215]. Through performance-based contracts and relying on an arm's length basis, agencification was born with the intention of 'giv[ing] managers sufficient space to get on with management'[216] giving them 'flexibility in the allocation of financial and human resources in return for greater accountability for results'[217].

While the creation of agencies or *agencification* pre-dates the 1980s' rise of New Public Management (NPM), going back over three hundred years[218] and contrary to its supporters' claim, it is with the advent of NPM that agencification became a government household means for innovation[219]. Despite the absence of an uncontroversial definition of what is meant by 'agency', a general consensus has been reached on what is meant by 'agencification', as well as the fundamental characteristics of an 'agency' and its core functions.

Bokhorst and Cleuren (2009)[220] recognize that '[s]cholars are often divided on the [issue of agencification]...[T]he different views fit into the traditional fault lines of, on the one hand, the supporters of NPM, privatization, and liberalization who state that bureaucratic control suffocates initiatives and is counterproductive and, on the other hand, those who state that the public administration is now beyond the effective control of democratic institutions in many Western countries.'

Driving factors

Simply put, '[a]gencification refers to the creation of semi-autonomous organizations[, structurally disaggregated and binded through performance contracting[221]] that operate at arms' length of the government, to carry out public tasks (regulation, service delivery, policy implementation) in a relatively autonomous way'[222] 'to improve, in some way, how government works'[223].

Agencification entails 'a transfer of government activities to agency-type organizations vertically specialized outside ministerial departments'[224]. At the centre of agencification lies the agency. While a universal and clear definition of 'agency' has not been reached owing to the wide 'range of organisations which have been termed 'agencies'', Talbot and Pollitt (2000)[225] identify five characteristics that make an entity in fact an 'agency'. To be called so, an 'agency' must (i) be at arms' length from the central ministry, (ii) carry out public tasks at a national level, (iii) core staffed by public servants, (iv) financed by state budget, and (v) subject to at least some public or administrative law procedures. The pool of characteristics also calls for an 'agency' to be (vi) binded by contractual arrangements – target setting, monitoring, and reporting[226], and (vii) enjoying a distinctive degree of autonomy[227].

Agencies are established to (i) make decisions about grants and contracts as a means of insulating these decisions from direct political control; (ii) regulate economy and society; (iii) provide expert policy advice; (iv) engage in information gathering and dissemination; (v) carry out research; (vi) function as tribunals and public enquiries; and (vii) provide representational and participatory opportunities for segments of the civil society[228].

As the principal characteristics of agencification – *structural disaggregation* and *performance contracting* – fall within NPM's 'doctrinal components'[229], it is not surprising to have witnessed a rise in agencification at the height of NPM, for NPM 'placed agencification high on the agenda of administrative policy-makers'[230].

Structural disaggregation provides essentially a form of functional specialization. Talbot and Pollitt (2000)[231] see it as a means to 'unbundle bureaucracy' breaking up policy-makers (purchasers) from policy-implementers (providers). Seen as an advantage, disaggregation translates into 'a [focused] single or few purposes agency...that in turn, tends to raise expertise, quality and efficiency'[232].

The second core notion associated with agencification is *performance contracting*. Talbot and Pollitt (2000)[233] sustain that with contractual arrangements, results are clearly reflected as outputs and outcomes and that, if well-designed, contracts 'can minimize foreseeable problems in the principal-agent relationship' while, at the same time, 'allow[ing] agency management the maximum discretion as to the means' towards achieving contracted results.

A direct relationship exists between structural disaggregation and performance contracting. As the former 'alone is unlikely to produce rapid change in the productivity or outlook of an organization', the latter 'is likely to work less well in the absence of parallel structural disaggregation'[234].

In line with the underlying principles of NPM, Talbot and Pollitt (2000)[235], sustain that agencification addresses shortfalls that affect legitimacy, rationalization, and delivery. From a political standpoint, they argue, establishing agencies 'has been seen as a method of revitalizing the legitimacy of public institutions [as well as 'lessening political influences over activities']...in the eyes of an increasingly skeptical and apathetic citizenry'. From a policy perspective, agencification 'specifies more clearly the goals and means of policy delivery and...create[s] more 'strategic' tools for policy-making' thus improving allocative efficiency. And, in terms of administration or management, they argue, agencification provides the means to rid the system of '[c]logged-up bureaucracies' and replace them with 'more flexible, responsive, [revitalized, focused, performance-oriented, transparent,] customer-friendly public services'.

While it may be difficult to generalize, a further advantage of agencification is its geographical neutrality in certain cases. 'Location', Egeberg and Trondal (2010)[236] argue, 'seems to be unrelated to agency autonomy, agency influence and inter-institutional coordination because of the efficiency of modern communication and transportation.' Even more interesting is how the finding is contrary to the argument by practitioners 'that physical distance might serve to underpin the intended autonomy of agencies from political executives'[237]. In fact, Egeberg and Trondal (2010)[238] argue that 'the considerable weight assigned to signals from affected interested groups and the parent ministry is clearly not contingent upon agency site.' However, they also recognize that in cases where the agency is more involved in providing inputs to the political-making process then being 'on the spot means that many actors and arenas can be reached in a relatively short time'[239]. Further, they also appreciate the 'symbolic effects' of visibility and reach as well as the more pragmatic provision of additional professional job opportunities borne from 'geographical dispersion of [central government's] institutional apparatus'[240].

Effectiveness

While many authors have readily equated agency with better performance, Talbot and Pollitt (2000)[241] recommend caution and feel it is 'yet totally inadequate.' They also caution about the universality of agencification as each adaptation comes with baggage. Albeit Talbot and Pollitt (2000)[242] argue in favor of disaggregation and performance contracting as being 'internationally portable', they also argue that 'disaggregation only makes sense in those countries which have experienced large, multi-functional bureaucratic organisations'. They further sustain that performance contracting appears to be less understood in Mediterranean and central European states than generally Anglophone countries as the former 'still conceive…[public administration] primarily as an activity of applying the law...rather than as a business of trying to achieve a publically-specified set of outputs or outcomes.'

The advantages claimed by agencification are based on the principle that it provides governments with the means to improve public functions delivery based on autonomy, flexibility and performance. Achieving a less hierarchical organizational structure, where managers are free from political influence is in itself a great result when juxtaposed to a degenerated bureaucratic *modus operandi*. This can be achieved through establishing agencies at arms' length of the government. The mere establishment of agencies, however, becomes just an output and an end it itself. *Goal displacement*[243] tells us that meeting the target (*e.g.* agency creation) is not necessarily a guarantee the underlying objective (*e.g.* improving the lives of citizens by carrying out public tasks in an efficient and effective way) will be likewise met. As with regards to any other government decision, in the case of agencification, the aim is not to lose sight of the agency's basis for existence and the deficiencies it is trying to address.

Moyhinan (2006)[244] argues 'that public management ideas that carry the same label[, in this case agencification,] can mask variation in the understanding of the policy, the motivation for adoption and in implementation outcomes.' To best illustrate ambiguities in agencification, Moyhinan (2006)[245] makes references to 'the oldest source of experiential information about agencies [*i.e.* Sweden,]...and a transitional country that received less attention in public management research, Slovakia.'

Contrary to supporters' claim of NPM doctrine, Sweden is the country with the longest track record on agencification, dating back to the 1700s[246]. With a small central government, 'practically all state services are performed by agencies enjoying considerable autonomy'[247]. In Sweden, 'the power of the ministers and the government to issue orders for agencies is constitutionally circumscribed', meaning 'individual minister[s and Cabinet] are prohibited to issue orders...[and] the agency is to be guided only by the law'[248]. This means that agencies' autonomy is constitutionally protected from political interference. The 'soft governing' typical of the Swedish public administration left politicians set the agenda and agency executive run the daily work 'with extensive discretionary authority' and 'at a considerable distance'[249].

However, '[t]he agencies have become too autonomous in relation to their political superiors…and their ability and willingness to work together in order to solve common problems have decreased'[250]. Laking (2002)[251] argues that the Swedish model's '[m]ost prominent criticism…was that the efforts to ensure administrative independence had succeeded too well, with ministries struggling to provide adequate oversight and direction, and agencies enjoying a strong information asymmetry over the centre.' By 2002, the number of agencies in Sweden rose to approximately 300 with around 222,000 employees, overseen by approximately 5,000 ministry employees, or a ratio of 1:45[252]. With such imbalance, agencies have been able to maintain autonomy[253].

While the Swedish agency model clearly emphasizes the schism between policy and implementation and between political influence and managerial discretion, which are important elements of the NPM, Swedish 'agencies became associated with inefficient government and excessive independence'[254]. With a relatively weak centre, Swedish agencies dominate bureaucratic control[255]. While at least satisfying the *autonomy* requirement, the supposedly intended beneficiaries of the agencies' work have not necessarily seen the results. Moynihan (2006)[256] argues, in fact, that 'experience of Sweden suggests that agencification did not improve responsiveness to citizens;…that agencies became well-organized constituencies to protect the policy *status quo*;…[and] that policy coordination was difficult'[257].

With regards to the experience of transitional countries, Slovakia, once independent, placed agencification low on the policy agenda *vis-à-vis* its focus primarily on decentralization[258] despite seeking 'public management policies consistent with democratic market system and [seeking to address] demands involved in becoming a member of the EU'[259]. The reason for Slovakia's regard towards agencification as a low priority has historical roots in its communist past. Paradoxically, the communist party was ahead regarding principles now inherent with modern NPM. Owing to the impossibility of controlling all aspects of production and daily life, the central communist party heavily relied on public entities, 'often enjoying significant discretion in budgetary and personnel matters[260]. Beblavy (2002)[261] argues that during the communist era agencies were characterized as a 'chaotic free-for-all,... [with] often legally defined autonomy, [where] their staff and particularly managers [felt] certain informal ownership rights and the distinction between public- and private-sector mentality [was] blurred or non-existent in the eyes of most actors.' To make matters worse, a general audit in 2000 identified as many as 150 agencies [including both pre- and post-independence] with only 22 ministries and warned that the total number of existing agencies had been already 'raised beyond a manageable limit...result[ing] in the non-transparency of the entire central state administration'[262].

Agencification in Slovakia was characterized primarily by 'the lack of a strong central actor to define any public management issue beyond decentralization...[and by] the ambiguity of the administrative recommendations of the most critical external stakeholders, the EU'[263]. Considering the gap between capacity assumed by NPM and local realities, Verheijen (1997)[264] argues that while 'NPM ideas might well be useful,...they should be carefully tailored to local circumstances.' While [a]gencification allowed for increases in or formalization of bureaucratic autonomy and the extension of services without obvious tax increases... [it] has shown little concern with the issues of improved performance or accountability'[265]. This was particularly due to the motivation surrounding agencification in Slovakia. Personal aggrandizing interests by actors were at the same time twinned with a 'focus...on serving party interests or demands of the EU, leading to an *ad hoc* response rather than a coherent framework for agency design'[266]. Particularly on external demands, Slovakia needed 'to satisfy the AcquisCommunitaire, the

basic conditions for joining the EU'[267], one of which being the creation
of new agencies as part of the accession process'[268]. In line with goal
displacement, performance (*i.e.* improving services for the benefit of
its citizenry) took a back seat to the mere creation of agencies for the
purpose of meeting personal motivations as well as both internal and
external political pressures. The agencification experience in Slovakia,
therefore, witnessed the provision of significant authority to agencies
without strong controls and performance frameworks, information
asymmetry, and political influence, resulting in serious problems of
corruption, accountability, weak incentives for performance, and a weak
capacity for a central strategic coordination of cross-cutting policies[269].
The potential for such abuse subsequently lessened not much because
of a later introduction of performance framework but rather the greater
political control and oversight over agencies by the central government[270],
in line with Tanzanian reformers approach of 'hand off – eyes on'[271].

Ten years ago or so, Talbot and Pollitt (2000)[272] argued the 'jury [was]
still out on' whether agencies really worked. Ten years later or so, van
Thiel *et al.* (2009)[273] argue that '[e]valuation studies show…the objectives
of agencification are not always achieved, and that there are unintended
consequences. The rise of unelected…agencies…has created problems
for the democratic accountability of ministers in parliament [as citizens
lose direct control of elected policy makers], and has on occasion led
to preserve outcomes such as corruption, underperformance, loss of
control and coordination, financial scandals, and so on.'

Ironically, while NPM advocates for a 'leaner, and increasingly privatized
government, emulating not only the practices but also the values of
business'[274], the number of administrative agencies rose, enlarged
the scope of government, expenditures increased[275], duplication of
expenditures also increased[276], and created more bureaucratic leadership
positions[277].

Concluding remarks

Speculating whether advantages of agencification outweigh disadvantages rests on the empirical determination of whether, by creating a specialized agency, the government is in a better position to carry out its inherent functions in a more efficient and effective way. If the government's objective is simply to appease the public or external political actors by showing they indeed created an agency, then this would represent just a cosmetic fix. While it serves as a first required step, the physical presence of an agency alone is no indication of delivery improvement. Moving away from a potential goal displacement, if on the other hand, the true *ends* of producing results is achieved, then any disadvantage would be outweighed. However, '[d]espite the potential benefits of...agency creation, there is need for governments to exercise caution. Experiences...suggest that agencies require the existence of a credible system for monitoring performance and ensuring financial accountability before relaxing control over inputs. Where controls are weak..., introducing greater managerial flexibility may only increase arbitrary and corrupt behaviour'[278].

While recognizing 'the mushrooming of agencies' as a result of the public service effort to create 'structures and systems to enable horizontal coordination', OECD[279] likewise recognized that 'the public service remains segmented overall, leading to suboptimal coherence in policy development, implementation and service delivery''. As agencification brought about 'fragmentation, duplication, weak regulation of democratic accountability', evidence shows that 'governments have embarked on programmes of rationalization and reassertion of central controls, referred to as post-NPM'[280]. Nonetheless, rather than calling for a termination of agencification as a whole, 'it advocated a more managed process of agency creation and greater use of 'shared services' between agencies, including mergers if warranted'[281].

While deficiencies in the agency performance exist, disadvantages can be remedied. OECD thinks so. It is not necessarily clear, however, whether the lives of the citizenry, which should be the fundamental focus of any government intervention, have actually been improved. If citizens' lives have improved, despite known organizational disadvantages, then it is worth retaining the services of agencies. The government can then work on improving and strengthening its monitoring and oversight functions over the work of the agencies.

Chapter Six

Decentralization

If participation of citizens and local governments is to exist and/or is to have an impact on lives of people, in line with current democratization trends, then creating an environment conducive to such decision-making and involvement in public affairs is essential. According to Rondinelli (1981)[282] 'decentralization has been advocated as a way of eliciting that participation' in favour of a more democratic governance and as a means to 'break the grip of central government'[283].

The principle of decentralization is based on a number of factors aimed at facilitating better governance, including better resource allocation closer to the point of delivery and therefore 'more efficient to provide public good and services tailored toward the preferences and tastes of individual residents',[284] less interference by central government in local implementation, enhanced empowerment of local government, enhanced accountability for results, and strengthened administrative and financial skills of local government officials[285].

While aiming to provide greater responsiveness to its citizens, Dilliger (1994)[286] argues that important decentralization reform warrants '(a) clarity in functional responsibility between levels of government; (b) authorization of revenue sources corresponding to functional responsibilities, and (c) institutionalization of a system of accountability that encompasses both regulations by central government and incentives for responsiveness to local constituents.' This approach is important and necessary taking into account a mixed set of result with the implementation of decentralization reforms. This outcome is further supported by many studies on decentralization, one of which was commissioned by USAID in 2010. The comparative study of decentralization processes across ten countries in Africa in major areas such as stability, democracy, development and service delivery, in fact, reveals 'modest improvements...as a consequence of decentralization'[287].

Efforts towards decentralization are important despite the generally resounding lukewarm results; they are important because of decentralization's sheer potential if done properly and within an understood context.

The chapter addresses underlying theoretical frameworks on decentralization and the relation of decentralization particularly with accountability, corruption, and effectiveness of local governments.

Theoretical frameworks

Decentralization of powers, responsibilities and resources from central to local governments can be categorized into three dimensions – political, administrative, and fiscal – and four typologies – devolution, deconcentration, delegation, and privatization[288]. No one is apparently disputing these distinctions.Whether we are discussing centralized or decentralized governance, at least three underlying theoretical frameworks provide a minimum of rationale in addressing both accountability and corruption.

The *principal-agent theory*[289] addresses the relationship between elected politicians (principals) and bureaucrats (agents), between political intent and administrative practice, and in turn between citizens (principals) and the elected politicians (agents). In essence, the theory heavily captures delegation from principal to agent, agent's interpretation and compliance *vis-à-vis* principal's will, monitoring and control on the part of the principal of the agent's actions, accountability mechanisms, and information exchanges, particularly asymmetric information. The theory indiscriminately applies to matters of accountability, corruption, and effectiveness in public activities.

According to *public choice theory*, citizens, politicians and bureaucrats 'are guided by self-interest in choosing the course of action to their best advantage'[290]. '[V]oters are deemed to vote for parties and candidates that will best serve their interests in terms of the rewards they expect to receive from governments. Politicians…[will] offer policies that will win them voters' support [thus gaining 'income, power and prestige derived from being in office']…Bureaucrats' self-interest leads them to maximize their budgets because larger budgets are a source of power, prestige, perks, and higher salaries'[291]. Self-interest potentially promotes rent-seeking behaviour among actors in the political process, obfuscates accountability frameworks, and undermines the realization of public goods and services aimed at benefiting the public as a whole.

Becker's *crime-and-punishment model* also contributes to the explanation of corruption, in particular. The model is based on the principle that 'an individual [will] compare the expected utilities of legal and illegal behavior, [and will opt for illegal behaviour when the latter]…is positively related to the potential gains from illegal activity and negatively related to the probability of conviction and…punishment'[292].

Accountability

Decentralization is believed to promote accountability of local governments. This is based on a number of principles, among which (i) being closer to the people, local governments are more aware of the preferences of the people; (ii) being closer to local governments, people are more aware of the works of local governments more so than the national programmes and can more directly demand services that better reflect their preferences; (iii) people can vote local official out; and (iv) people can vote with their feet.

As sustained by Gurgur and Shah (2000)[293] and others, '[t]here is a general agreement in the literature that [decentralization] can open up greater opportunities for voice and choice thereby making the public sector more responsive and accountable to citizens-voters.' Seabright (1996)[294] argues that accountability is always better at the local level, since local citizens who are better informed about government performance can vote these governments out of office. This reinforces, therefore, the accountability of local governments to its principals, the people.

However, it is not always the case that information exchange is strengthened with decentralization; media coverage must play its part for it to be effective. Local governments are not always more accountable than central governments. A study by the University of Maryland on the decentralization of health and education services in the Philippines and Uganda found that asymmetric information, coupled with limited authority, undermined accountability in both countries. In both countries, the people were more informed about national programmes than those of the local governments, mainly because they relied on media for information, which focused more on the national government and limited its coverage of politics and events at local level[295]. Similarly, particularly in the Philippines, only municipal officials [rather than provincial officials] were aware of [local preferences]'[296]. Lack of relevant information and limited citizen's participation are relevant ingredients that contribute to lack of accountability.

With greater availability of ground-level information, coupled with competition for resources and constituents, local governments are 'considered to be most responsive to the variations in demands for and costs of providing public goods' to individuals[297]. This is particularly due to the threat of jurisdictional mobility ('voting with feet') exercised by the constituents to other jurisdictions or private and non-governmental organizations should tailored needs not be met by public goods and services provided by their local governments[298]. According to Tiebout (1956)[299], 'consumer-voter moves to that community whose local government best satisfies his set of preferences [for public goods]'. It is much easier said than done, however. There are cases, in fact, where jurisdictional mobility would not exist at all. It would not be an option for citizens or a threat for governments as in the case of 'economic dependency of a landless tenant on the feudal lord' in the rural Sindh province of Pakistan[300]. Haque (1997)[301] argues that local-level accountability is undermined by 'the prevalence in inequality in local power structure.' This is particularly evident in rural areas in 'Asian, African, and Latin American countries...characterized by a feudal or semi-feudal structure of property ownership composed of the elitist land owning class, small farmers, and landless peasants'[302]. This means that 'the accountability of local institutions often remains an accountability of the local elites rather than to the ordinary people such as the marginal and landless farmer'[303].

The question whether local governments are more accountable to their people due to decentralization is even more so undermined when the former is not accountable to either the people or central government. This is the case of the local forest governance in Indonesia. With decentralization, coupled with lack of 'appropriate devolution processes or control mechanisms', local governments enjoyed the spoils of opportunistic behaviour[304]. After 1998, power and authority over local forestation was decentralized to district governments. Rather than stop illegal deforestation and granting permits, district officials colluded with private loggers backed by military and police personnel to the detriment of conservation areas and the environment – *i.e.* increased occurrence of flooding and landslides[305]. Decentralized authority and usurpation by district official of such authority resulted in a degenerated grand scheme whereby district officials find themselves 'less accountable to the public of the central government than they are to the private business interests that support their elections and contribute to their official district revenues as rent from extracted forest resources'[306]. Owing to the 'disastrous [decentralization] process leading to the destruction of large production forests, conservation forests, and nearly all of the national parks in Jambi', the central government issued a new regulation interpreted to be 'an effort to re-centralize power and authority'[307].

Corruption

Based on a literary review conducted by Fjeldstad (2004)[308], 'relatively few studies have been carried out that explicitly focus on the linkages between decentralization and corruption' and 'theoretical studies point in different directions and provide no-clear cut conclusions on the linkages between decentralization and corruption'.

Crook and Manor's (2000)[309] studies of India, Bangladesh, Cote d'Ivoire, and Ghana reveal that 'decentralization leads to enhanced transparency. With enhanced transparency, ordinary citizen become better aware of government's successes and failures and they may perceive the government institutions more corrupt that the perception they had before.' This does not say much, however, whether corruption increased in absolute terms. It could be that the level remained the same, only now citizens are more aware of corruption because of the transparency brought about by decentralization. Moreover, as we will see in the case of New York City school boards below, decentralization not necessarily leads to transparency.

In the vein of conflicting accounts, while Breton (1996)[310] argues that 'competition between levels of government will lead to less corruption', Banfield (1979)[311] concludes that 'decentralised political systems are more corruptible, because the potential corrupter needs to influence only a segment of the government, and because in a fragmented system there are fewer centralized forces and agencies to enforce honesty.' Reduced 'willingness to monitor' by higher-tier officials due to the loss of control does not favour its containment[312]. '[T]here are more opportunities for corruption at the local level' owing to the resulting greater discretionary powers by local officials...and pressures directly from local interests groups[313].

Supporters of decentralization like Wade (1997)[314] argue 'that India's top-down structure was largely responsible for corruption in the irrigation bureaucracy.' Also, Fisman and Gatti (2002)[315] found that a negative correlation exists between fiscal decentralization and corruption, more precisely that the former is 'consistently associated with lower measured corruption'. Their study revealed 'that countries with more decentralized expenditures have better corruption ratings'[316]. Brueckner (1999)[317], on the other hand, sustains 'that corruption is more likely to be a problem among local governments. Furthermore, in contrast, Bardham and Mookherjee (1998)[318] 'find that the relationship between decentralization and the extent of rent extraction by private parties is ambiguous.'

New York City's experience with the decentralization of public schools was so negative to the point that in 1997 the City reversed its 1969 decentralization law because of abuses[319]. While the intent of decentralization mirrored the widely accepted principle for its adoption – the desire to bring government closer to its constituents – its unintended consequence was 'widespread and systematic corruption' at the hands of '[a] majority of the city's 32 school boards [that] carved their districts into fiefdoms where jobs were doled out to loyal campaign workers, lovers, and family or sold for cash'[320]. While 'the widely shared, long-range goal was always to improve education[, f]ew anticipated the extent to which schools would be turned into patronage mills'[321]. With decentralization and minimal oversight, board members had discretion to hire principals, non-pedagogical employees, and control promotions of teachers but not their hiring[322]. In line with Becker's *model of crime-and-punishment*, a structure was created where it was 'so easy to engage in [corruption] and get away with it, and where the rewards for corrupt behaviour [were] so great, that the system invite[d] it and, in a number of districts, necessitate[d] it'[323]. Owing to the absence of media scrutiny of school board meetings and elections, low voter turnouts, secret meetings, and the fact that the chancellor could not remove them from office, board members were practically insulated from educational accountability[324]. In terms of effectiveness of New York's experience with school decentralization, '[d]istricts most beleaguered by patronage rank[ed] lowest in citywide test scores', per capita spending was the lowest for teachers 'who did not provide local boards with patronage', less resources were spent on the classrooms, academic qualifications of

superintendents was not a determinate factor in the hiring, governments
services and morale were harmed[325].

Effectiveness

The argument about the 'effectiveness' of public services depends
on whether we measure (i) the delivery of services as planned by the
government *in direct response* to the public preferences or (ii) the
delivery of services as planned by the government that *do not necessarily
respect* the preferences of the public. The issue has separate implications.
One could possibly look at the claim made by Walsh (1995)[326] that '[t]
he introduction of local management seems to have led to significant
increases in the level of administration of [British] school[s]' as reflective
more of the latter claim. Walsh's uncertainty 'over whether the devolution
of finance actually [did] anything to improve the standard of education,
would stem, instead, more emphatically from a direct preference of the
people.

Effectiveness of decentralization depends on design and implementing
institutional arrangements (citizens' voice mechanisms, exit
mechanisms, central government laws, rules, budget constraints,
oversight bodies, accountability management arrangements)[327]. The
same study by the University of Maryland[328] on the decentralization
of health and education services in the Philippines and Uganda that
was highlighted above under 'Accountability', also assessed whether
allocative and productive efficiency were achieved. The study found
that local officials had 'limited authority to adjust services' and their
degree of 'corruption was less pronounced…than at national levels'[329].
Nonetheless, the effectiveness particularly of immunization program in
Uganda was found to be limited because of decentralization. Specifically,
while 'the central government…delivers vaccines to health facilities,
local governments have been made responsible for funding outreach
programs to immunize children and pregnant women. But local
governments do not always view immunization as a priority,…[they
also view it as] a low priority for additional government spending'[330].

In developing countries, however, evidence 'that decentralization promotes demand responsiveness of government services' is limited and not necessarily 'tailored to local demand'[331]. On the one hand, research conducted by Bird, Ebel and Wallich (1995)[332] in Eastern and Central Europe suggests a negative effect of decentralization on public services. Decentralization created, according to Winkler and Rounds (1996)[333], inequities in expenditures in Chilean schools. On the other hand, Matheson and Azfar (1999)[334] argue that improvements in health and education in the Philippines materialized as a result of decentralization. In a study conducted by Isham and Kahkonen (1999)[335] on community-based water services in Central Java, decentralization improved services but only when 'users themselves were directly involved in service design and selection'.

Civil society participation in local government also influences the outcome of local policies and programs. Putnam (1993)[336], for instance, 'demonstrated that Italian regions in which the public actively participates in civic activities are also the regions in which local governments exhibit higher performance…with respect to the delivery of public services.' In a study on ethnic diversity in city governments in the United States, Alesina, Baqir, and Easterly (1999)[337] concluded that ethnic diversity reduces the performance of local public services. While this finding supports the argument by Olson (1982)[338] that 'the ethnic group in power…limit[s] the spending on public goods to prevent those outside the ruling group from also benefiting and getting stronger', it also supports the inference that American city governments are then, by default, operating at a reduced performance given the ethnic diversification of American society including public authorities.

While Treisman (2000)[339] recognizes the existence of corruption at both levels of government, data 'collected…on up to 154 countries…suggests that states which have more tiers of government tend to have higher perceived corruption, and may do a worse job of providing public health services. Federal states appear less effective at providing public health services and (at least among developing countries) at lowering adult illiteracy.'

Concluding remarks

Opportunities and risks are seen differently in the eyes of supporters and critics of decentralization. Decentralization is 'perceived both as a solution to problems such as dysfunctional public sector, lack of voice and exit as well as source of new problems such as capture by local elite, aggravation of macroeconomic management due to lack of physical discipline and preserve physical behaviour by sub-national units'[340], sometimes to a point where steps were taken to 're-centralize' once decentralized functions, as in the case of New York City's school boards and Indonesia's forest resources management.

Evidence on decentralization remains mixed. Owing to the various conclusions drawn on the relationship between decentralization, accountability, corruption, and effectiveness the contention of whether decentralization makes local governments more accountable, less corrupt, and more effected than central governments remains conclusively unanswered, but not unanswerable. As recognized by scholars, a great deal of additional empirical evidence is required to conclusively support either claim. In the meanwhile, despite the attractiveness of its principles, greater care is needed in 'defining and contextualizing decentralization', by taking into account 'the degree of socioeconomic development and size of a country…[,its] existing degree of responsive governance [, t]he immediate political circumstances underlying decentralization…[as well as] a greater understanding of the subnational context [including]…how policy processes and decision-making takes place at the local level.'[341] In other words, proceed but with caution.

Chapter Seven

Corruption

Overwhelmingly, corruption is recognized as 'an insidious plague that has a wide range of corrosive effects on societies'[342] as it compromises 'the stability and security of societies, undermin[es] the institutions and values of democracy, ethical values and justice and jeopardiz[es] sustainable development and the rule of law'[343].

This chapter addresses theoretical literature on corruption and what it tells us about how corruption should practically be combated. In this light, the chapter aims to answer the following questions – (i) Whichtheories have been developed for combating corruption? (ii) Which of these theories actually works in practice? More specifically, the aim is not to address which theoretical framework works *always*, as there is no evidence to support this universality, but rather to address those that have proven to have worked in reducing corruption. In order to address these questions, there is a need first, albeit very briefly, to define *what* we are trying to combat and *why* we are trying to combat it in the first place. In so doing, the chapter will also address general underlying causes of corruption.

Definition, causes, and consequences

While negative consequences of corruption to society are widely shared by theorists and practitioners, it is also evident they have not reached a formal and unanimous agreement on its definition. The *United Nations Convention Against Corruption* of 2003 is a case in point. After two years of deliberations, though Member States signed the Convention, the term '"corruption" was not defined at all'[344]. While corruption 'is readily understood and readily applied everywhere, there is hardly any agreement on where precisely the boundary between a corrupt and non-corrupt act should be drawn'[345]. The difficulty in unanimously defining the phenomenon stems from the reality that what may be regarded as corrupt behavior in one country may not necessarily be regarded so in another.

While variations of the working definition of corruption sum up to the 'abuse of public office for private gains'[346], it should be recognized that '[c]orruption…also exists within and between private business and within non-governmental organisations, without any state agency or state official being involved'[347]. Therefore, albeit not addressing corruption in the private sector in this chapter, a more inclusive working definition of corruption should capture 'the misuses of a public or private position for direct or indirect personal gain'[348].

It is widely recognized, however, that 'corruption is a symptom of deep-seated economic, political and institutional weaknesses'[349] and the result of too much monopoly and discretion and less accountability[350]. Simply put, economic enablers stem from low public sector wages and, as such, corruption is grossly influenced by the attractiveness of pecuniary gains. In some countries, wages are so low that it is practically 'impossible for an honest civil servant to subsist on his salary alone…[which could] last…little more than a week'[351]. With regards to the political dimension, corruption is attributed to the greed for additional power whereby top officials may organize the state to enrich themselves[352]. Institutional weakness exists when there is excessive red tape, unclear rules and processes, inhospitability to foreign trade, poor accountability mechanisms, poor citizen participation, poor awareness and informational and educational campaign, poor media or no freedom of the press. As highlighted by empirical evidence, corruption is less when 'there are fewer trade restrictions; where governments do not engage in favoritist industrial policies; where natural resources are more abundant; and where civil servants are paid better, compared with similarly qualified workers in the private sector'[353].

While corruption is not by any means unique to poor countries, 'it is in the developing world that its effects are most destructive...by diverting funds intended for development, undermining a Government's ability to provide basic services [particularly education and health], feeding inequality and injustice and discouraging foreign aid and investment'[354]. Empirical evidence supports the position that '[c]orruption...distort[s] the composition of government spending...[where c]orrupt politicians... spend more public resources on those items on which it is easier to extract large bribes [such as]...on fighter aircraft and large-scale investment projects [rather] than on textbooks and teachers' salaries, even though the latter may promote economic growth to a greater extent than the former'[355]. Furthermore, corruption affects the 'growth that is expected...to come from private investment. Rent seeking... increase[s] the costs associated with entrepreneurial investment and may lead foreign investors to take their business elsewhere. Corruption also forces domestic entrepreneurs to go underground, leading to high levels of informality and a narrow tax base'[356].

Theories on combating corruption

Theories for combating corruption fundamentally address prevention, deterrence, and education pillars. The theory that best serves anti-corruption preventive efforts and that which is consistently addressed in the literature reviewed is Klitgaard's (1998)[357] analytical framework on corruption '$C=M+D-A$'. Applying the reverse logic, then, would provide us with a workable theory against corruption. Monopoly, discretion, and accountability are the three aspects to address. Corruption could be reduced or eliminated by reducing the monopoly power over goods and services politicians and bureaucrats possess, limit and clarify their discretion to decide who gets the goods and services, and increase transparency and accountability to ensure all see what they have decided[358]. Reducing monopoly means limiting the benefits under the purview of public officials and opening the market to competition by 'lower[ing] the controls of foreign trade, remov[ing] entry barriers for private industry and privatis[ing] state firms'[359]. Reducing discretion means increasing incentives and remunerations comparable to politicians and bureaucrats' equivalents in the private sector[360] as well as simplifying administrative procedures[361]. Transparency and accountability aspects include citizen oversight mechanisms where there is an increased public access to information, also through computerized data systems, as well as increased participation public budget hearing programme and planning[362].

As corruption is a crime of calculation which matures 'when risks are low, the penalties mild, and the rewards great'[363], deterrent measures need to focus on 'increasing the probability of detection, apprehension and conviction and the penalties of malfeasant behaviour'[364]. The term 'frying the big fish' is essential according to Klitgaard et al. (2000)[365] to break the culture of corruption and increase credibility; example of which is the punishment in Hong Kong of a former police of Hong Kong who was extradited from retirement in England[366]. In the case of Singapore, its deterrent and enforcement measures are quite stiff. In fact, whether a person did or did not receive a bribe and if found to have committed the gratification, the person is to pay the full amount plus other punishment imposed by the court; in the event the person is not able to pay in full, a stiffer sentence will be imposed. Singaporeans that live and are involved in the crime abroad are also subject to the same penalties[367].

As sustained by Boehm (2007)[368] and essentially many others, 'corruption breeds in opacity: in a crystal clear world of perfect information there would be no possibilities to abuse existing rules in order to derive benefits for own pockets.' As per Deininger and Mpuga (2004)[369] '[e]conometric analysis confirms that households' knowledge on reporting corruption is indeed a key factor in reducing their susceptibility to being asked to pay bribes.' Moreover, Klitgaard (1998)[370] argues that 'citizens are fertile sources of information about where corruption is occurring' and should be both consulted and made aware through a series of measures that include 'systematic client surveys; setting up citizens' oversight bodies for public agencies; involving professional organizations; consulting with village and borough councils; and using telephone lines, call-in radio shows, and educational programs', as well as freedom of the press.

Political will is *sine qua non* to any anti-corruption effort. Study cases below reflect this key enabler. While the success of the case of Hong Kong highlights political will, one should be mindful that establishing anti-corruption commission is not an automatic indication of genuine political will 'if political leaders are only responding to demands from international donors...ignor[ing] domestic demands for reform and enact minimal reforms to satisfy external agents'[371]. A second caveat relates to resource availability. While some approaches are certainly more expensive than others (*e.g.* universal anti-corruption commissions *versus* citizen engagement), one should beware from 'wast[ing] a million to steal a thousand'[372]; in other words, the costs involved in anti-corruption initiatives should not outweigh the benefits.

Theories that work in practice

Anti-corruption agencies or commissions of Hong Kong and Singapore are the more influential representatives, more known and visible means to fighting corruption. Of the two, this chapter addresses Hong Kong's Independent Commission Against Corruption (ICAC). Recognizing the need for a 'well thought out and comprehensive strategic plan' rather than a single solution, ICAC adopts a three-pronged approach that covers deterrence, prevention and education[373]. Following this approach, in its first 25 years ICAC was able to 'smash...all corruption syndicates in the Government and prosecute...247 government officials, including 143 police officers. [ICAC's approach e]radicated all the overt types of corruption...[c]hanged the public's attitude to no longer tolerating corruption as away of life; and support the fight against corruption and are not only willing to report corruption, but are prepared to identify themselves in the reports'[374]. Furthermore, 'over 2,000 private companies have sought corruption prevention advice in areas like tendering, procurement, and staff administration...The majority of [private companies as well as trade and professional associations] are now putting [ICAC] codes into practice with training seminars organized with...ICAC's assistance...Also, about 7,000 managerial and front-line staff of 1,700 small and medium size companies have received preventive educational training'[375]. ICAC's success is based on its three-pronged approach mentioned above[376]. Deterrent measures include an effective public complaint system (including complaints against ICAC), a quick response system, zero tolerance policy, exposing corruption through media coverage, and a strong enforcement policy. At the same time, preventive measures focus on specialized professional staff, staff integrity, streamlining procedures, checks and control frameworks, organizational efficiency, transparency, and accountability. The education approach is equally important and it focuses on media publicity, media education, school ethics education programme from kindergarten up to the universities, seminars, exhibitions, fairs, television variety shows to spread the message of a clean society, and websites. ICAC is fully supported by top political leaders, operates as a truly independent agency within a comprehensive legislation to deal with corruption, and it is fully resourced.

Following the principles of Klitgaard (1998) analytical framework for corruption (C=M+D-A), in 2001 Bolivia's National Tax Service focused on *institutional* reforms to reduce corruption by reducing discretion and increasing accountability[377]. While collecting taxes remains part of the government's monopolized function, it is yet possible to tackle the other two elements in the equation. Discretion was reduced with the adoption of 'a new centralized information technology system [that includes] an on-line tax collection system through the commercial bank network'[378]. Further measures included intensive training, merit-based hiring practices, streamlining of norms and procedures, as well as improved inspection and control processes. These institutional measures resulted in a reduction of tax evasion by approximately one third over the period 2001-2004[379].

As a preventive measure, the New York Police Department carries out yearly random and targeted *integrity testing*, which is a measure to '[d]etermine whether or not a particular civil servant or branch of government is likely to engage in corrupt practices'[380]. The practice is well publicized among the police force and entails 'creat[ing] scenarios based upon known acts of police corruption' and are monitored and recorded through audio-visual surveillance. With yearly targeted testing on about 4 percent of officers, where there is a suspicion of foul play, evidence would indicate that only '[a]bout 20 per cent...fail the test' and 'only about one per cent' of those randomly tested failed. 'This would seem to support the long held view of senior NYPD management that the vast majority of its officers are not corrupt'[381]. The London Metropolitan Police has followed suit by adopting 'a similar programme of integrity testing...and early reports indicate that they are obtaining some of the same benefits'[382].

Providing citizens easy access to information is by far an inexpensive proposition when compared to other major government programmes as discussed above, as well as being crucial to a bottom-up approach. The use of *public hearings* in rural India, for instance, is found to be an effective measure 'to root out corruption at the local level and demand accountability from the development establishment'[383]. By exercising the people's right to information, a 'public hearing in the small village of Lasani, revealed how Rs.56,000 was...spent to construct water channels [which existed only on paper] linking the village...pond... with the fields'[384]. In another village, 23 completed development works were examined during a public hearing in the village of Surajpura and found a wide range of frauds, including variances between actual and reported wages paid, the same contractor's name appearing in multiple muster rolls, and the name of a contractor who had deceased some thirty years earlier[385].

In Uganda, citizens were empowered when the government initiated a *newspaper campaign* aimed at 'reduc[ing] district-level capture of a public program aimed at increasing primary education'[386]. The government 'began to publish data on monthly transfers of capitation grants to local governments (districts) in newspapers'[387]. In an effort to promote accountability under this programme, teachers and parents were given 'access to information on...[school] entitlements and the workings of the grant program'. Both were therefore put in a position to 'monitor the local administration and voice complaints if funds did not reach the schools'[388]. The programme was also serious on cracking down 'on officers found to be misusing public funds...[and]signaled strengthened oversight by the central government...[Under these circumstances then d]istrict authorities...knew they would be held accountable for any shortfall (or at least understood that the likelihood of this happening had increased)'[389]. As a result, 'capture was reduced from 80 percent in 1995 to less than 20 percent in 2001'[390].

The work of Transparency International (TI) is an example of a successful campaign for *raising public awareness* on citizens' rights and *citizen empowerment* at no expense to the government. TI's Advocacy and Legal Advice Centers (ALACs) are grass roots empowerment *mechanism* that 'provid[e] citizens with assistance in filing and pursuing corruption related complaints'[391]. Through a three-pronged approach – educative, curative, and preventive – ALACs projects (funded by the German Foreign Ministry and implemented by TI) aim to raise public awareness on citizen rights 'among the stakeholders who are critical to the anti-corruption struggle: the state, the media, civil society and, most importantly, the citizenry itself'[392]. *Educative* strategy entails 'the provision of information and the building of public awareness so that citizens not only become aware of their rights with regard to corruption, but feel empowered to demand their rights'[393]. The educative approach includes a telephone hotline, face-to-face meetings, website, a 'how to' essential citizen's guide, a library of publications, a database, and media coverage, including radio, television and print[394]. The *curative* approach entails 'the exercising of citizen rights in terms of the competent investigation and resolution, by public authorities or state-sanctioned anti-corruption mechanisms, of cases where citizen rights have been violated'[395]. Lastly, *prevention* entails promoting 'legal and institutional reform designed to prevent or minimize corruption chiefly through the passage of new laws, regulations or mechanisms and/or modifications to or improved compliance with existing legislation'[396]. An evaluation of ALACs in Romania, Macedonia, and Bosnia and Herzegovina[397] finds 'that the project has been highly successful...[where a] high portion of the clients interviewed held the opinion that their cases would not have progressed at all without ALAC assistance'. The public profile of TI has grown considerably in these countries to a point where, according to a Romanian journalist, '[t]he Government pays a lot more attention' to TI's and ALACs' work and 'have been actively soliciting TI advice and expertise in their own reform efforts.' TI's 'advocacy efforts...have attained a greater impact than originally envisioned, especially in terms of legislative and policy reform initiatives [including having] been consulted on pending Conflict of Interest and Freedom of Information legislation...[and in Romania] has had considerable success in influencing – or even being asked to help draft legislation such as the new Whistleblower's Protection Act'.

Concluding remarks

While no single and universal definition of corruption has been reached, generally three approaches are recognized in combating corruption – prevention, deterrence, and information. The underlying success depends on a number of factors, among which are political will and resource availability. Measures that tackle corruption include holistic approaches (*i.e.* ICAC) and those that predominantly focus on creating and taking advantage of citizen awareness and empowerment (*i.e.* ALAC). Countries that cannot afford holistic measures, might wish to limit their focus within a limited field (*e.g.* Bolivia's tax administration). While the work of both ICAC and ALAC heavily tackle the information/ education approach, the promotion of citizen involvement, empowerment and awareness appears to behave positive results for less advantaged countries as well (*i.e.* India and Uganda).

michael anthony

tarallo

Chapter Eight

Public Resources

Management of public money is at the foundation of any functioning government. While so, it is the quality of such management that brings about conditions for effective delivery of services to the public. Its management is by no means a simple undertaking and requires at a minimum political commitment, institutional and individual behavioral change, and the institutionalization of a cross-the-board approach to result-oriented budgeting and management.

This chapter focuses on resource availability, transparency, and elements of public expenditure management, as experienced by five developed countries and ten developing countries.

Money matters

Owing to lack of own resources, most developing countries are heavily dependent on foreign capital inflows[398]. Can poverty itself be a major factor for poor performance in developing countries? Schick argues that 'being poor has a lot to do with unwanted outcomes'[399]. While poverty certainly contributes to deficiencies in public expenditures management, being *kept* into poverty by international lending institutions, however, cannot certainly be helpful to lesser advantaged countries.

While rich in resources, Africa, for instance, remains indisputably a poor continent and a poorly run one. The environment within which public resources are managed is exacerbated by overwhelming external public debt. Over a period of thirty years since the 1970s, Africa alone paid over 88 percent of its accumulated loans just in interest. Africa remained with a bill equaling 78 percent of its original loan yet to be paid[400]. The severe conditionality imposed by international lending institutions on macroeconomic frameworks has had a destructive consequence to developing countries, particularly concerning social sectors[401]. For instance, en face the ravages of HIV/AIDS, Malawi found itself two-thirds short in the total number of nurses required and a 90 percent short in total number of required doctors. Despite this critical deficiency in human capacity, Malawi was not 'allowed to hire more staff and pay better salaries, because it would breach the macroeconomic' policies imposed by the International Monetary Fund[402]. Institutional conditionality has had a negative impact on education in Malawi as well. Though recognized by the United Nations System as 'the ultimate vector of human progress', accessibility to primary education is rendered unattainable by imposed education fees[403]. These are the same fees borne from structural adjustment policies of the World Bank[404]. In situations like these, resources that should have been used for socio-economic growth are actually tied down to the repayment of accumulated debt. This conditionality is by all means a non-starter to progress and development.

Developed countries as well are not void of financial pressures. After all, considering both developed and developing countries accumulated a combined debt of over $36 trillion in 2010[405], it is hard to fathom developed countries being shielded from financial pressures alike. The only difference is that developed countries have more flexibility and borrowing power than developing countries, and as such, it is expected they would eventually be in a position to sanitize their fiscal balance.

As in the case of external debt, budget deficits signal 'shortcomings in the management of public expenditures'[406]. Owing to the lack of resources, even developed countries have shown to operate in the same manner developing countries do. The United States alone, for instance, faced in 2010 a $3 trillion budget deficit because of the effects of the recession and reckless allocative decisions made by previous administrations[407].

Drawing from an approach prevalent in developing countries, whereby cash is spent only when available[408], in his States of the Union address, President Obama called upon 'the Senate…[to] restore the pay-as-you-go law'. This approach 'was a big reason for why [the United States] had recorded surpluses in the 1990s'. This approach enables countries 'to maintain fiscal discipline despite their economic straits'[409].

Further to debt and deficits, discussion on money matters warrants attention to revenues. Predicting the availability of resources is driven by the ability of a country to actually collect taxes. A good degree of revenue predictability makes financial management much more manageable. Among the developed countries reviewed, Norway's taxpayers' registration, tax assessment, and tax collection, is highly effective[410]. In the United States, however, efforts are being concentrated on cracking down on tax evasion by hiring about 2,000 new dedicated employees 'expected to increase tax collection by $26 billion over the next ten years'[411]. In Jamaica, while tax payer's registration is good, collection is not[412]. The Dominican Republic's experience, on the other hand, impressively showcased a tax default rate less than 1 percent in 2007[413]. The decline in public revenues is both a challenge and a priority in the Philippines[414]. Local governments are unable to collect the full potential revenues. This is primarily due to inaccurate tax registration, inaccurate information on property taxes, large numbers of non-filers and non-payers, poor audit presence for business taxes, inadequate levels of trained professional staffs, inadequate data on payment delinquency, cash-based payment system, and no taxpayer services[415].

Transparency

Schick (1998)[416] argues developing countries are characterized by 'systemic corruption, lax tax administration, informal markets, and misguided regulations.' The question he poses, however, is whether such characteristics are the cause of poverty or actually the effect. Poor countries are indeed more 'susceptible to these deficiencies because they are poor.' While 'poverty generates dysfunctional institutions,' it is also fair to say, Schick argues, that 'dysfunctional institutions keep countries poor'[417].

In both developed and developing countries, confidence and trust in government by the public is threatened by perceived and corroborated cases of corrupted politicians and government officials and widespread cronyism[418]. 'Government corruption', Rizvi argues, '...hinders development and perpetuates poverty...caus[ing] 40 per cent of the population in Asia and Africa to live below the poverty line'[419]. In the Philippines alone, it is estimated that the cost of corruption in the last twenty years amounted to $48 billion; resources that could have been allocated to public services and goods[420].

There is more to corruption, however, than just the association to poverty. Culture, in fact, appears to have an impact on its severity. In some developing countries, culture has shown to bring about opposite results concerning corruption. Ethiopia and the Philippines are a case in point. Respectively, Ethiopia and the Philippines ranked 86th and 48th in the global gross domestic product (GDP) in 2008[421]. Philippines's GDP is six times that of Ethiopia. It is apparently "the disciplined culture of the Ethiopian society, which does not encourage corruption" and which lends to 'no evidence of a systemic and widespread corruption in the Government sectors'[422]. This is so even *en face* low civil servants remuneration[423]. Philippines' political culture, on the other hand, tends to tolerate corruption. Poor civil service remuneration, favoritism and gratitude repayment for electoral campaign support, poor control and enforcement mechanism, weak public oversight, bureaucratic red tape, and information asymmetry make of corruption a widespread phenomenon[424].

None of the four developed countries (Australia, Norway, New Zealand, and the United States) under review are characterized by a widespread presence of corruption. One should not, nonetheless, be under any impression that developed countries are left immune from corruption and interference. This is evidenced by recent measures taken by the

United States. To support transparency and to curtail lobbyist pressure and interference, the United States began posting all visitors to the White House online and excluded lobbyists from government positions. It is further intended to require full disclosure on contacts with politicians and contribution made by the lobbyists, in clear contraposition of the Supreme Court's recent ruling on lifting limits to election contribution by domestic or foreign special interests[425].

Transparency is not limited to the presence or not of corruption but rather it includes the availability and accessibility of information to the public. Moreover, the quality of the information, its presentation, and its reporting all affect the degree of transparency.

In Norway, accessibility by the public is reported to be good[426]. Similarly, six countries of the Organisation of Eastern Caribbean States (OECS) are reported to have good public access to budget, accounting and audit reports[427]. Jamaica has an historical tradition of 'a vibrant public oversight of the government's financial management'[428]. In the United States, as well, information on budgets, audits, government debates, public affairs is quite accessible to the public in person or through televised, electronic, and printed media. In Ethiopia, on the other hand, public's access to information is not easy and no comprehensive guidance exists on gaining access to such information[429].

Delayed reporting exacerbates transparency. This is the case in six OECS countries. While the accessibility is reportedly good, reporting to the legislature is generally delayed and not comprehensive as it omits aid funding[430]. Bad records management in these countries also contributes to a compromised transparency as it undermines the administration, auditing, and the veracity of financial statements[431]. In Ethiopia, as well, in addition to donor funds not reflected in the budget and in financial statements, the actual reporting is delayed[432]. In the Philippines, there is an extensive use of special funds that do not necessarily align with national priorities and, as they occur in off-budget years, such funds are not accounted for in either the budget formulation or during implementation[433]. The introduction to accrual budgeting and accounting as well as to output and outcome budgeting system in Australia is reportedly to have weakened transparency and parliamentary control, at least when first implemented. On the one hand, this is owed to the lack of understanding and competency of the legislature[434]. On the other, while the switch to output and outcome budgeting has given the flexibility to managers to decide the best mix of resources, in so doing, it has made it difficult to track where the money actually goes owing to the frequent changes to the plan[435].

Public budgeting

Public budgeting[436] as a whole is a vital management instrument borne from a long and complex strategic decision-making process that serves public administrators as a fundamental instrument in the formulation of policies and strategies. Aside from steering internal coordination in the budgeting formulation and the implementation control, budgets are also regarded as legal contracts between the executive and the legislative branches of governments specifically with regards to mutually imposed obligations concerning the raising of (taxation) and expenditure of public funds. Further, fiscal policy relies also on budgets to stimulate or slowdown national economic growth by increasing or decreasing taxation as well as revenue expenditures. A further characteristic, as Rubin posits, is that 'public budgets are not merely managerial documents [for imposing control, economy, and efficiency in government]; they are also intrinsically and reducibly political,'[437] for they reflect power play, bargaining, and negotiations of various entities involved in the budgeting process. Lastly, budget documents are also a means to public accountability, where all entities in government are set to be held accountable for their actions in terms of the budgeting process and the finite overall performance of the economy. In simple terms, budgeting is at the same time the means and the result of a labor-intensive organizational strategic planning that is based on previous experience, new executive direction and associated requirements, and competing political influences.

One of the most important decision processes in government's decision-making, budgeting systems have evolved to reflect many problems; these include shortsightedness, fragmentation, and a preoccupation with process rather than results. These problems heavily contribute to incongruence between budget process and budget content[438]. Friedman argues that the first characteristic problem of a modern budget is that it suffers from shortsightedness. Most budgets run a one or two-year budget cycle and, this being the case, little emphasis is placed on decision-making that spans for a longer timeframe. This, therefore, limits the systematic consideration and evaluation of long-term trends. Shortsightedness presents difficulties because very rarely the problems government services aim to resolve will have a limited duration of only year or so. This means, also, that one and two-year funding cycles encourage short-term solutions and most offices involved in the budgeting process very seldom have either the expertise, time, or willingness to develop information systems that support long-term strategic planning[439].

The second general problem with the budgeting process is that it is unavoidably subject to procedural fragmentation. There is a plethora of funding committees and subcommittees involved in the process with very little synchronization among them or interest in what the other is doing. 'Government organization is often a maze of interrelated, overlapping and sometimes duplicative structures...[that]...tend to carve up and compartmentalize problems, rather than dealing with whole problems.'[440] The end result is that making comprehensive and coherent decisions with regards to funding requirements and subsequent allocations becomes both cumbersome and difficult. At the very end, the *impact* on incurred expenditures suffer.

The third identified problem posits that "budgeting systems tend to be slavishly devoted to process rather than results."[441] The focus is centered primarily on the process itself, on what government entities do, and on tracking the level of expenditures incurred. But very little interest, or at least not until recently, is dedicated to gathering and analyzing the impact of government activities and services delivered to the citizenry. Budgeting systems with no regard to the outcomes may be considered successes in terms of procedural achievements but failures in terms of the accomplishments and the attainment of socially driven goals.

It follows that essentially three management and budgeting focus frameworks exist, (i) input-focused, (ii) output-focused, and (iii) outcome-focused framework. The first two frameworks center on the level of resources – *i.e.* personnel, funds, facilities, and equipment – made available to the organization to carry out its activities, and on the level of products and services being delivered, respectively. Neither of the two frameworks, though, evaluates the achievements brought about by the implementation of resources (input) and the deliverance of finite products and services (output).With the aim of achieving a system that would effectively ensure better performance and accountability, public administration's focus has shifted to a new form of performance budgeting – one that focuses on the *impact* of organizational activities rather than on activities and outputs as witnessed with the performance budgeting of the 1950s. In the 1990s, the new development came to be known as *new performance budgeting, outcome-based budgeting*, or *results-based budgeting*.

The whole budgeting philosophy has therefore changed. With outcome budgeting, agency and program managers are forced to think beyond the immediate concept of resources, activities, workload statistics, or the number of benefit recipients. This new budgeting system promotes a greater vision of accomplishment by requiring executives to ask what tangible difference governmental programs are actually making in the lives of the citizenry. As a result and, at the same time, as a means of achieving programs' objectives, greater emphasis is placed on system-wide planning, strategy, implementation, and budgetary control. Furthermore, by clearly linking results with funding levels, outcome budgeting fosters accountability and increased transparency in both the decision-making process and policy implementation.

The natural consequence is that results are not limited to the budgeting process alone but rather to the entire management approach to the operationalization of daily administrative functions as well as to the determination of the overall impact of the organization's work. A results-based management system is a mechanism that forces politicians, bureaucrats, and voting citizens to be clearer about the objectives of government programs and services so as not to lose sight of their purpose, which is to serve the public[442].

Public expenditure management

As noted above modern public expenditure management is geared towards increasing the probability of achieving results. This depends on a strong aggregate fiscal discipline (institutional framework, control of budget aggregates, rules, procedures, and budgetary ceilings), flexibility to reallocate resources in line with reengineered priorities, as well as operational efficiency in the provision of services to the public[443]. Developing countries tend to be challenged in all three structural pillars of public expenditures management[444]. What obstacles, then, keep developing countries from progressing in the management of public resources? There are a number of reasons contributing to this deficiency. Lack of capacity in the legislature, the executive, as well as in the accounting and auditing functions is a major challenge. This is particular due to inadequate training, high turnover and shortage of staff, and not competitive remuneration which hinders the ability to attract and retain qualified staff. All six countries of the OECS reviewed[445], as well as Ethiopia[446] and the Philippines[447] suffer from one or more of the preceding shortcomings. In countries like Ethiopia[448], there is no regulatory body for the accounting and auditing profession. In the Philippines, the accountancy profession is regarded as 'one of the world's most vibrant'[449]. This means that quality is not necessarily the only requirement for a well-functioning internal control and oversight functions but rather it is a combination of statutory frameworks, skills, job satisfaction, and availability of manpower.

An added burden to public expenditures in developing countries is the actual size of the civil service, albeit generally low paid, with generally low entitlement spending[450]. Large size of the civil service translates in huge allocations of public resources. In the Philippines alone, for instance, the significant fiscal burden varies between 35 percent at national level and 75 percent in the province of Negros Occidental[451].

Developing countries operate in a highly unstable and unpredictable environment. It is because of this environment that Schick prescribes longer timeframes within which to formulate single year budgets[452]. On the negative side, single year budgets facilitate deferment of expenditures to future years; in so doing, distorting current years account presentations and, at the same time, hindering the achievement of future targets. On the positive side, with multi-year frameworks, politicians are less probable to break fiscal discipline. Schick also advocates the institutionalization of spending limits[453].

In Australia, a medium-term expenditure framework 'has eased the inevitable frictions of budgeting and has permitted the government to finance new priorities while slowing the growth rate of public spending'[454]. In New Zealand, such framework contributed to the reduction of public debt[455]. Sweden put a similar multi-year framework to address recurring budget deficits, lax budgetary procedures and a recession[456]. Norway[457] and the United States[458] as well operate within multi-year with clear and well defined roles, and they operate within a budgetary ceiling.

Out of the developing countries, multi-year frameworks are followed in the Philippines[459], and, out of the six OECS countries, only in St. Lucia[460]. Jamaica formulates its budget within a funding ceiling nonetheless the credibility of the budget is rather weak. Individual government agencies' estimates, in fact, reflect for the most part a needs list which considerably exceeds the available resources. Arrears are paid out of future year's budget[461].

Developing countries operate amidst systemic inefficiencies. 'The lack of predictability', argues Schick (1998)[462], '...discourages managers from making investments that will yield high productivity in the future.' The experience in the developed world, instead, reflects a greater focus on future planning and spending. Social spending, for instance, on welfare, health care, and labor productivity are at the forefront of public political debate. Nonetheless, this focus does not come without its challenges.

One of New Zealand's challenges to fiscal management is its heavy spending on social welfare. As compared to other OECD countries, unemployment insurance is generous and provided for longer-term unemployment. One of the efforts to reduce social spending has been to invest in training programs and create jobs[463]. In Australia, the economy and social expenditures are affected by the rise in public health, long-term care, public pensions, and low labor productivity owed to an ageing population over the next twenty years[464]. To counter this pressure, policies are geared towards increasing productivity growth and labor inputs through incentives to join the labor force, incentives to late retirement, incentives to a return to work by increasing benefits to encourage older workers to accept low paying jobs[465]. In the United States, faced with high unemployment, where one out of ten is out of work, efforts were focused on creating conditions for business expansion and increased hiring. Measures include the reallocation of identified $20 billion dollars in savings for the 2011 budget, the $30 billion that has been already repaid by Wall Street banks, and a government spending freeze for the next three years starting in 2011[466].

Concluding remarks

A number of factors have direct influence in the proper management of public expenditures. The availability of resources is most certainly a major factor that affects both developing and developed countries, but to different degrees. The development of poor countries is impaired, among others, by their debt repayment obligations to international lending institutions. To address heavy deficits, developed countries like the United States turn to tactics that are generally typical of developing countries. The predictability and collection of tax revenues are a common challenge for both groups of countries. Lack of predictability influences future spending.

While developing countries are discouraged by long-term planning and spending, the reverse occurs in developed countries, instead. It is generally recognized that remuneration of the civil service in developing countries is low compared to that in the private sector and, as a whole, due to the size of the civil service required remunerations constitute a considerable percentage of public resources. Low salaries tend to lead to dissatisfaction, poor performance, and corruption, as well as to the inability to attract and retain skilled professionals. This problem was evidenced in all developing countries reviewed.

Those few developing countries operating in multi-year expenditures frameworks with spending limits prove that following these structures is not enough if allocative and operational efficiency of Schick's public expenditures management are not in place. Allocative and operational efficiency are just as important as aggregate fiscal discipline. In their absence, particularly the allocative flexibility, results can be significantly damaging. 'When they fund ineffective programs,' Schick (1998)[467] argues, 'developed countries obtain suboptimal returns on public expenditure…When poor countries misallocate resources, development is retarded and poverty persists.'

ENDNOTES

Chapter One – Introduction

[1]   Tarallo (2012)
[2]   Dunleavy, *et al.*, 2005, p.437
[3]   Drechsler, 2005
[4]   Bourgon (2003) cited in Bourgon 2007, pp.8-9
[5]   Metcalfe, 1998, cited in Yamamoto, 2003, p.4
[6]   Pollitt, 1995, cited in Vabo, 2009, p.3
[7]   Haque, 2007, p.179
[8]   Yamamoto, 2003, p.4
[9]   Hood (1991), pp.3-5
[10] Osborn and Gaebler (1992), cited in Vabo, p.3
[11] Denhardt and Denhardt, 2000, p.549
[12] Dunleavy *et al.*, 2005, p.477
[13] Gershon, 2004, cited in *ibid.*, p.483
[14] Wise, 2002, cited in Dunleavy *et al.*, 2005, p.481
[15] *ibid.*, p.482
[16] Gregory (2007), cited in Vabo, 2009, p.18
[17] Dunleavy *et al.*, 2005, p.467
[18] *ibid.*
[19] Haque, 2007, p.179
[20] Dunleavy *et al.*, 2005, p.468
[21] Haque, 2007, p.179
[22] Dunleavy *et al.* (2005), p.468
[23] Talbot (2008), p.3
[24] *ibid.*, p.8
[25] *ibid.*, p.9
[26] Talbot (2008), p.3
[27] Alford and Hughes (2008), p.131
[28] Moore, 1995, cited in *ibid.*
[29] Echebarria, 2001, cited in Drechsler, 2005

[30]   Howlett, M. and Ramesh, M. (2003), pp.120-121

[31]   Jenkins, 1978, cited in *ibid.*, p.6

[32]   Howlett, M. and Ramesh, M. (2003), p.7

[33]   *ibid.*, p.12

[34]   *ibid.*, p.13

[35]   *ibid.*

[36]   cited in *ibid.*, p.14

[37]   *ibid.*

[38]   Sabatier, 1992, cited in *ibid.*

[39]   Kingdon, 1984, cited in *ibid.*, p.120

[40]   *ibid.*, p.121

[41]   Surel, 2000; Snow and Benford, 1992; Steinberg, 1998, cited in *ibid.*

[42]   Hogwood and Gunn, 1984, cited in University of Birmingham, 2010b, pp.21-22

[43]   cited in Howlett and Ramesh, 2003, pp.132-133

[44]   University of Birmingham, 2010b, p.18

[45]   Howlett and Ramesh, 2003, p.143

[46]   *ibid.*, p.133

[47]   cited in *ibid.*, pp.133-134

[48]   cited in *ibid.*, pp.135-137

[49]   *ibid.*, p.143

[50]   cited in *ibid.*, pp.175-176

[51]   cited in *ibid.*, p.176

[52]   cited in *ibid.*, p.137

[53]   Howlett and Ramesh, 2003, p.138

[54]   Dye, cited in *ibid.*, p.123

[55]   *ibid.*, p.124

[56]   cited in *ibid.*, p.129

[57]   cited in *ibid.*, p.131

[58]   cited in Hudson and Lowe, 2004, p.117

[59]   cited in University of Birmingham, 2010b, p.21

[60]   cited in Hudson and Lowe, 2004, pp.117-118

61 Howlett and Ramesh, 2003, p.16

62 Immergut, 1992, p.63

63 University of Birmingham, 2010b, p.71

64 cited in *ibid.*, pp.72-73

65 *ibid.*, p.73

66 Immergut, 1992, p.63

67 cited in Hudson and Lowe, 2004, p.157

68 *ibid.*, p.158

69 cited in Howlett and Ramesh, 2003, p.140

70 Hudson and Lowe, 2004, pp.142-143

71 Nunan, 1999, p.621

72 *ibid.*, p.636

73 Marsh and Smith, 2000, p.4

74 *ibid.*, p.5

75 *ibid.*

76 *ibid.*, p.8

77 Daugbjerg, 1996; Van Waarden, 1992, cited in Nunan, 1999, p.621

78 cited in Hudson and Lowe, 2004, p.132

79 cited in Howlett and Ramesh, 2003, p.139

80 Baumgarten and Jones, 1991, cited in *ibid.*

81 Marsh and Rhodes, 1992, cited in *ibid.*, p.134

82 Howlett and Ramesh, 2003, p.5

83 cited in Hudson and Lowe, 2004, pp.135-136

84 cited in Howlett and Ramesh, 2003, p.52

85 Hudson and Lowe, 2004, p.123

86 Considine, 1998, p.312

Chapter Three – Policy Transfer

87 Page, 2000, p.2

88 Stone, 1999, p.57

89 *ibid.*

90 Rose, 1991, p.9

91 *ibid.*, p.5

92 Stone, 1999, p.53

93   Gonzalez, 2007, p.1

94   Dolowitz and Marsh, 1996, p.344

95   Dolowitz and Marsh, 2000, p.13

96   Rose, 1991, p.6

97   Hudson and Lowe, 2004, p.166

98   Dolowitz and Marsh, 2000, p.7

99   Hudson and Lowe, 2004, p.163

100 *ibid.*

101 Lewis, 2005, p.5

102 *ibid.*, p.15

103 *ibid.*, p.14

104 Hudson and Lowe, 2004, p.39

105 Rose, 1991, p.11

106 Stone, 1999, p.54

107 DiMaggio and Powell, 1983; Teague, 1999, cited in Page, 2000, p.8

108 Gonzalez, 2007, p.2

109 Stone, 1999, p.54

110 Kenis, 1999, cited in *ibid.*

111 Rose, 1991, p.11

112 Kingdon, 1984, cited in Howlett and Ramesh, 2003, pp.135-137

113 Hudson and Lowe, 2004, pp.16-17

114 *ibid.*, p.17

115 Evans and Davies, 1999, p.371

116 Cerny, 1992, cited in *ibid.*

117 *ibid.*

118 Oduwaye, 2006, p.199

119 Srivastana, 2004, cited in Gonzalez 2007, p.6

120 Gonzalez, 2007, p.3

121 PEGR, 2005, cited in *ibid.*

122 Gonzalez, 2007, p.5

123 *ibid.*

124 PEGR, 2005, cited in *ibid.*

125 *ibid.*

126 Gonzalez, 2007, p.6

127 Wilson, 2003, cited in *ibid.*

[128] *ibid.*, p.7

[129] *ibid.*, p.6

[130] *ibid.*, p.7

[131] Evans and Davies, 1999, p.376

[132] *ibid.*, p.377

[133] Stone, 2000, pp.66-67

[134] *ibid.*, p.52

[135] cited in Ladi, 1999, p.9

[136] Youde, 2005, p.1

[137] *ibid.*, p.20

[138] *ibid.*,p.7

[139] Pierson, 2003, p.95

[140] Peck and Theodore, 2001, p.431

[141] *ibid.*

[142] Dolowitz, 2000, p.374

[143] Hudson and Lowe, 2004, p.164

[144] Evans and Davies, 1999, p.363

[145] *ibid.*, p.364

[146] James and Lodge, 2003, p.184

[147] Dolowitz and Marsh, 2000, pp.13-14

[148] James and Lodge, 2003, p.185

[149] Dolowitz and Marsh, 2000, p.6

[150] James and Lodge, 2003, p.183

[151] Evans and Davies, 1999, p.382

[152] Dolowitz, Greenwold, and Marsh, 1999, p.719

[153] Bennett, 1997, cited in Stone, 1999, p.52

[154] *ibid.*, p.56

[155] *ibid.*, p.52

[156] Dolowitz, Greenwold, and Marsh, 1999, p.729

[157] Nedley, 2004, p.165

[158] *ibid.*

[159] Merton, 1940, p.56

[160] *ibid.*, p.564

[161] *ibid.*, pp.562-563

[162] *ibid.*, p.563

[163] Child, 2005, p.9

[164] Alexander, 1976, pp.182-183

[165] Kerr, 1975, p.769

[166] Warner and Havens, 1968, p.539

[167] *ibid.*, p.541

[168] Davies, 1999, p.155

[169] *ibid.*

[170] Perrin, 1990, cited in *ibid.*

[171] Davies, 1999, p.155

[172] Alexander, 1976, p.183

[173] *ibid.*, p.184

[174] *ibid.*

[175] *ibid.*, p.188

[176] *ibid.*

[177] *ibid.*, p.189

[178] Pressman and Wildavsky, 1973, cited in *ibid.*

[179] Abramson, 2009, p.65

[180] *ibid.*, p.66

[181] *ibid.*, p.69

[182] *ibid.*, p.74

[183] Goldsmith

[184] *ibid.*

[185] *ibid.*

[186] Kerr, 1975, p.769

[187] *ibid.*, p.772

[188] *ibid.*

[189] *ibid.*, p.773

[190] *ibid.*

[191] Walker, 2009, p.3

192 Kohn, 2000, cited in *ibid.*, p.5

193 Linn, 2000, cited in *ibid.*, p.6

194 *ibid.*, p.8

195 *ibid.*, p.9

196 *ibid.*, pp.9-10

197 Bohte and Meier, 2000, p.5

198 *ibid.*, p.18

199 *ibid.*, p.19

200 Brehm and Gates, 1997, cited *ibid.*

201 cited in Stribu, 2008, p.25

202 Stribu, 2008, p.25

203 United Nations, 2010

204 Stribu, 2008, pp.30-31

205 *ibid.*, p.26

206 Sundaram, 2007, cited in *ibid.*

207 Elson, 2004, cited in *ibid.*

208 Stribu, 2008, *ibid.*

209 Merton, 1940, p.564

210 Child, 2005, p.103

211 *ibid.*, p.93

212 *ibid.*, pp.126-127

213 *ibid.*, p.127

214 Mayne, 2001, cited in Perrin, 2002, p.4

Chapter Five – Agencification

215 Batley and Larbi, 2004, p.45

216 Jervis and Richards, 1995, cited in *ibid.*

217 Batley and Larbi, 2004, p.45

218 Moynihan, 2006, p.1034

219 van Thiel *et al.*, 2009, p.12

220 Bokhorst and Cleuren, 2009, p.3

221 Talbot, 2004, cited in Ekelund, 2010, p.24

222 van Thiel *et al*, 2009, p.2

223 Talbot and Pollitt, 2000, p.2

[224] Egeberg and Trondal, 2010, p.1

[225] Talbot and Pollitt, 2000, pp.4-5

[226] Talbot, 2004, cited in Ekelund, 2010, p.24

[227] Bouckaert and Peters, 2004, cited in *ibid.*, p.26

[228] *ibid.*, pp.25-26

[229] Hood, 1991; Aucoin, 1990, cited in van Thiel *et al*, 2009, p.3

[230] Egeberg and Trondal, 2010, p.i

[231] Talbot and Pollitt, 2000, p.9

[232] *ibid.*, p.10

[233] *ibid.*

[234] *ibid.*, pp.16-17

[235] *ibid.*, p.2

[236] Egeberg and Trondal, 2010, p.12

[237] *ibid.*, p.2

[238] *ibid.*, p.8

[239] *ibid.*, p.12

[240] *ibid.*

[241] Talbot and Pollitt, 2000, p.13

[242] *ibid.*

[243] Merton, 1940

[244] Moyhinan, 2006, p.1029

[245] *ibid.*, p.1030

[246] *ibid.*, p.1034

[247] Jacobsson and Sundstrom, 2007, p.3

[248] *ibid.*, p.6

[249] *ibid.*, p.7

[250] *ibid.*, p.3

[251] Laking, 2002, cited in Moynihan, 2006, p.1034

[252] OECD, 2002, cited in *ibid.*

[253] Pierre, 2004, cited in *ibid.*

[254] Moynihan, 2006, p.1042

[255] *ibid.*

[256] Moynihan, 2006, p.1045

[257] *ibid.*

[258] SIGMA, 2002, cited in *ibid.*, p.1038

259 Moyhinan, 2006, p.1037

260 *ibid.*, p.1038

261 Beblavy, 2002, cited in *ibid.*, p.1039

262 INEKO, 2000, cited in *ibid.*, pp.1038-39

263 *ibid.*, p.1043

264 Verheijen , 1997, cited in *ibid.*

265 Moyhinan, 2006, p.1043

266 INEKO, 2000, cited in *ibid.*

267 Verheijen, 2003, cited in *ibid.*, p.1039

268 Moyhinan, 2006, p.1040

269 *ibid.*, p.1044

270 *ibid.*

271 Rugumyaheto, 2002, cited in Sulle, 2008, p.9

272 Talbot and Pollitt, 2000, p.15

273 van Thiel *et al*, 2009, p.3

274 Denhardt and Denhardt, 2000, p.549

275 Dunleavy *et al.*, 2005, p.477

276 Gershon, 2004, cited in Dunleavy *et al.*, 2005, p.483

277 Liegl, 1998, p.25

278 World Bank, 1997, cited in Batley and Larbi, 2004, p.46

279 cited in MacCarthaigh, 2010, p.21

280 *ibid.*, p.8

281 *ibid.*, p.21

Chapter Six – Decentralization

282 cited in Kim, I.S. (2007)

283 Olowy, 2000; Smoke, 1994; Wunsch and Olowu, 1990, cited in Fjeldstad, 2004, p.1

284 Karna, S.K. (2011)

285 University of Birmingham, 2010a, pp.65-66

286 cited in Karna, S.K. (2011)

287 Dickovik, J.T. and Riedl, R.B. (2010), p.6

288 Rondinelli and Nellis, 1986, cited in Karingi, 2003, p.2

289 Howlett and Ramesh, 2003, p.193

[290] McLean, 1987; Winden, 1988, cited in *ibid.*, p.22

[291] *ibid.*, p.23

[292] Gurgur and Shah, 2000, p. 7

[293] *ibid.*, p.4

[294] cited in *ibid.*, p.5

[295] World Bank, 2001, p.3

[296] *ibid.*, p.2

[297] Azfar, Kahkonen, Lanyi *et al*, 1999, p.2

[298] *ibid.*, p.3

[299] Tiebout, 1956, p.418

[300] Shah, 1998, p.21

[301] Haque, 1997, p.7

[302] *ibid.*

[303] *ibid.*, p.8

[304] Djogo and Syaf, 2003, p.1

[305] *ibid.*, pp.7-8

[306] *ibid.*, p.12

[307] *ibid.*, pp.12-13

[308] Fjeldstad, 2004, pp.2,4

[309] cited in Gurgur and Shah, 2000, p.5

[310] cited in Fjeldstad, 2004, p.4

[311] cited in *ibid.*

[312] Carbonera, 2000, cited in *ibid.*

[313] Prud'homme, 1995, cited in *ibid.*

[314] cited in Fisman and Gatti, 2002, p.2

[315] Fishman and Gatti, 2002, pp.2-3

[316] *ibid.*, p.6

[317] cited in *ibid.*, p.2

[318] cited in *ibid.*

[319] Segal, 1997, p.149

[320] *ibid.*, p.141

[321] *ibid.*, p.142

[322] *ibid.*

[323] *ibid.*, p.143

[324] *ibid.*, pp.144,146

[325] *ibid.*, p.147

[326] Walsh, 1995, p.176

[327] World Bank, 2001, p.1

[328] *ibid.*

[329] *ibid.*, p.2

[330] *ibid.*, pp.3-4

[331] Azfar, Kahkonen, Lanyi *et al*, 1999, p.4

[332] cited in *ibid.*

[333] cited in *ibid.*

[334] cited in *ibid.*

[335] cited in *ibid.*

[336] cited in *ibid.*, p.19

[337] cited in *ibid.*, p.20

[338] cited in *ibid.*

[339] Treisman, 2000, p.i

[340] Gurgur and Shah, 2000, p.2

[341] Fritzen and Lim (2006), p.8

Chapter Seven – Corruption

[342] Annan cited in United Nations, 2004a, p.iii

[343] United Nations, 2004a, p.2

[344] United Nations, 2004b, p.23

[345] Kurer, 2005, p.236

[346] Mauro, 1998, p.11

[347] Andvig, Fjeldstad, Amundsen *et al.*, 2000, p.14

[348] United States Treasury, cited in United Nations, 2004b, p.23

[349] Andvig, Fjeldstad, Amundsen *et al.*, 2000, p.140

[350] Klitgaard, 1998, p.3

[351] Robertson-Snape, 1999, p.593

[352] UNDP, 1997, p.1

[353] Van Rijckeghem and Weder, 1997, cited in Mauro, 1998, pp.11-12

[354] Annan, cited in United Nations, 2004a, p.iii

[355] Mauro, 1998, p.12

[356] Deininger and Mpuga, 2004, p.1

357 Klitgaard, 1998, p.4

358 Klitgaard, MacLean-Abaroa, and Parris, 2000, p.27

359 Ades and Di Tella, 1995, cited in UNDP, 1997, p.53

360 Ades and Di Tella, 1996, p.7

361 Gonzales de Anis, 2000, p.5

362 *ibid.*, pp.5-6

363 Klitgaard, MacLean-Abaroa, and Parris, 2000, pp.27,31

364 Ades and Di Tella, 1996, p.7

365 Klitgaard*et al*, 2000, p.79

366 *ibid.*

367 Quah, 2001, p.33

368 Boehm, 2007, p.3

369 Deininger and Mpuga, 2004, p.16

370 Klitgaard, 1998, p.4

371 Heilbrunn, 2004, p.1

372 Klitgaard, MacLean-Abaroa, and Parris, 2000, p.75

373 Kowk, 2006, p.196

374 *ibid.*

375 Yeung, 2000, pp.7-8

376 Kowk, 2006, pp.198-201

377 Zuleta, Leyton and Ivanovic, 2008, p.1

378 *ibid.*, p.12

379 *ibid.*, pp.11-13

380 United Nations, 2004b, p.89

381 *ibid.*, p.92

382 *ibid.*, p.93

383 Bathia and Dreze, 1998, p.1

384 *ibid.*

385 *ibid.*, p.2

386 Reinikka and Svensson, 2003, p.21

387 *ibid.*, p.3

388 *ibid.*, p.8

389 *ibid.*

390 *ibid.*, p.1

391 Keller-Herzog, 2006

392 McCarthy, 2005, p.2

393 *ibid.*, p.10

394 *ibid.*, pp.4-8

395 *ibid.*, p.10

396 *ibid.*

397 *ibid.*, pp.14-16

Chapter Eight – Public Resources

398 Schick, 1998, p.30

399 *ibid.*, p.6

400 Lewis, 2005, p.22

401 *ibid.*, p.5

402 *ibid.*, pp.14-15

403 *ibid.*, pp.74-75

404 *ibid.*, p.80

405 The Economist, 2010

406 Schick, 1998, p.3

407 Obama, 2010

408 Schick, 1998, p.37

409 *ibid.*

410 Norad, p.4

411 U.S. Treasury, 2010

412 European Commission, 2007a, pp.7-8

413 European Commission, 2007b, p.13

414 World Bank, 2003c, p.ii

415 *ibid.*,p.iii

416 Schick, 1998, p.33

417 *ibid.*

418 Rizvi, 2007, p.91

419 *ibid.*, p.107

420 Arugay, 2006

421 World Bank, 2009

422 World Bank, 2003b, p.37

423 United Nations, 2004c, p.12

[424] United Nations, 2004d, p.16

[425] Obama, 2010

[426] Norad, p.5

[427] World Bank, 2003a, p.47

[428] European Commission, 2007a, p.10

[429] World Bank, 2003b, p.41

[430] World Bank, 2003a, p.3

[431] *ibid.*, p.23

[432] World Bank, 2003b, p.24

[433] World Bank, 2003c, p.iii

[434] Scheers, Sterck and Bouckaert, 2005, p.139

[435] *ibid.*, p.150

[436] Excerpt from Tarallo (2004)

[437] Rubin (2000)

[438] Friedman (1995)

[439] Melaville (1997)

[440] Friedman (1995)

[441] *ibid.*

[442] Saldanha

[443] Schick, 1998, p.11

[444] *ibid.*, p.2

[445] World Bank, 2003a, pp.38-39

[446] World Bank, 2003b, pp.24, 29

[447] Asian Development Bank, 2002, p.11

[448] World Bank, 2003b, p.32

[449] Asian Development Bank, 2002, p.5

[450] Schick, 1998, p.73

[451] World Bank 2003c, p.x

[452] Schick, 1998, p.34

[453] *ibid.*, p.13

[454] *ibid.*, p.57

[455] OECD, 2002, p.2

[456] Schick, 1998, p.60

[457] Norad, p.3

[458] Lee and Johnson, 1994, p.135

[459]   Asian Development Bank, 2002, p.2

[460]   World Bank, 2003a, p.22

[461]   European Commission, 2007a, p.7

[462]   Schick, 1998, p.40

[463]   OECD, 2002, p.20

[464]   OECD, 2005, p.1,4

[465]   OECD, 1999, p.24

[466]   Obama, 2010

[467]   Schick, 1998, pp.93-94

michael anthony

tarallo

REFERENCES

Abramson, C.M. (2009) 'Who are the clients?: Goal displacement in an adult day care center for elders with dementia', *Int'l J. Aging and Human Development*, vol.68(1), pp.65-92

Ades, A. and Di Tella, R. (1996) 'The causes and consequences of corruption: A review of recent empirical conclusions', *IDS Bulletin*, vol.27 (2), pp.6-11

Alexander, E.R. (1976) 'Goal setting and growth in an uncertain world: A case study of a local community organization', *Public Administration Review*, (Mar-Apr 1976), vol.36 (2), pp.182-191

Alford, J. and Hughes, O. (2008) Public values pragmatism as the next phase of public management', *The American Review of Public Administration*, vol.38 (2), pp.130-148

Andvig, J., Fjeldstad, O-H., Amundsen, I., Sissener, T., Soreide, T. (2000) 'Research on corruption: A policy oriented survey', Chr. Michelsen Institute and Norwegian Institute of International Affairs [online] www.icgg.org/downloads/ contribution07_andvig.pdf [Accessed 2 August 2010]

Arugay, A.A. (2005) *From protest to participation? Accountability reform and civil society in the Philippines* [online] web.kssp.upd.edu.ph/talastasan/papers/arugay_protest_to_participation.pdf [Accessed 1 February 2010]

Asian Development Bank (2002) *Diagnostic study of accounting and auditing practices – The Philippines* [online] www.adb.org/Documents/Books/Diagnostic_Study_Accounting_Auditing/PHI/prelims.pdf [Accessed 3 February 2010]

Azfar, O., Kakonen, S., Lanyi, A., Meagher, P. and Rutherford, D. (1999) 'Decentralization, governance and public services: The impact of institutional arrangements: A review of the literature', IRSI Center, University of Maryland, [online] www1.worldbank.org/publicsector/decentralization/lit%20review%200999%20final.doc [Accessed 9 July 2010]

Batley, R.A. and Larbi, G.A. (2004) *The changing role of government: The reform of public service in developing countries*, Basingstoke: Palgrave MacMillan

Bhatia, B. and Dreze, J. (1998) 'Anti-corruption campaign in rural India' [online] unpan1.un.org.intradoc/groups/public/ documents/ apcity/ unpan013111.pdf [Accessed 27 July 2010]

Boehm, F. (2007) 'Anti-corruption strategies as safeguards for public service sector reforms', Working Paper [online] atom.univ-paris1.fr/documents/boehm_-_anti-corruption_as_safeguard_-_final_paris.pdf [Accessed 1 August 2010]

Bohte, J. and Meier, K.J. (2000) 'Goal displacement: Assessing the motivation for organizational cheating', [online] teep.tamu.edu /pubs/par01.pdf [Accessed on 11 November 2010]

Bokhorst, M. and Cleuren, H. (2009) 'Dutch government foundations: Between autonomy and accountability' [online] www.eur.nl/ fileadmin/assets/fsw/nig/workconf2009/ panel13paperbokhorstcleuren.pdf [Accessed 17 March 2011]

Bourgon, J. (2007) 'Responsive, responsible and respected government: Towards a New Public Administration theory',*International Review of Administrative Sciences*, 2007, vol. 73 (1) pp.7-26

Child, J. (2005) *Organization: Contemporary principles and practice*, Malden: Blackwell Publishing Ltd.

Considine, M. (1998) 'Making up the government's mind: Agenda setting in a parliamentary system', *Governance*, vol.11 (3), pp.297-317

Davies, I.C. (1999) 'Evaluation and performance management in government', *Evaluation*, vol.5(2), pp.150-159

Deininger, K. and Mpuga, P. (2004) 'Does greater accountability improve the quality of delivery of public services? Evidence from Uganda' World Bank Policy Research Working Paper 3277 (April 2004) [online] www.wds.worldbank.org/external/default/wdscontent server/iw3p/ib/2004/05/20/00000948620040520160455/rendered/pdf/wps3277uganda.pdf [Accessed 27 July 2010]

Denhardt, R.B. and Denhardt, J.V. (2000) 'The New Public Service: Serving rather than steering', *Public Administration Review*, 2000, vol.60 (6), pp.549-559

Dickovick, J.T. and Riedl, R.B. (2010) 'Comparative assessment of decentralization in Africa: Final report and summary of findings', USAID [online] www.pdf.usaid.gov/pdf_docs/pnadx211.pdf [Accessed 21 January 2012]

Djogo, T. and Syaf, R. (2003) 'Decentralization without accountability: Power and authority over local forest governance in Indonesia', [online] www.cifor.cgiar.org/acm/download/pub/djogo-ewc.pdf [Accessed 12 July 2010]

Dolowitz, D.P. (2000) 'The British Child Support Agency: did American origins bring failure?' *Environment and Planning: Government and Policy* (2001), vol.19, pp.373-389

Dolowitz, D.P. and Marsh, D. (2000) 'Learning from abroad: The role of policy transfer in contemporary policy-making', *Governance: An International Journal of Policy and Administration*, vol.3(1), pp.5-24

Dolowitz, D.P., Greenwold, S., Marsh, D. (1999) 'Policy transfer" Something old, something new, something borrowed, but why red, why and blue?'*Parliamentary Affairs*, vol.52, pp.719-730

Dolowitz, D. and Marsh, D. (1996) 'Who learns what from whom: A review of the policy transfer literature', *Political Studies*, vol.44 (2), pp.343-357

Drechsler, W. (2005) 'The rise and demise of the New Public Management' [online] www.paecon.net/paereview/issue33/ drechsler33.htm [Accessed 24 March 2011]

Dunleavy, P., Margetts, H., Bastow, S. and Tinkler, J. (2005) 'New Public Management is dead – Long live digital-era governance', *Journal of Public Administration Research and Theory*, vol.16, pp.467-494

Economist, The (2010) The Economist global public debt clock [online] buttonwood.economist.com/content/gdc [Accessed 7 February 2010]

Egeberg, M. and Trondal, J. (2010) 'Agencification and location: Does agency site matter? [online] www.sv.uid.no/arena/english/ research/publications/arena-publications/working papers/ working-papers2010/wp_03_10_online.pdf [Accessed 17 March 2011]

Ekelund, H.M. (2010) 'The agencification of Europe: explaining the establishment of European Community agencies' [online] etheses.nottingham.ac.uk/1269/phd_thesis_helena_ekelund. pdf [Accessed on 17 March 2011]

Evans, M. and Davies, J. (1999) 'Understanding policy transfer: A multi-level, multi-disciplinary perspective', *Public Administration*, vol.77 (2), pp.361-385

European Commission (2007a) *Final report on the PEFA assessment – Jamaica.* May 2007 [online] ec.europa.eu/europeaid/what/ economic-support/public-finance/documents/jamaica_pefa_ report_2007en.pdf [Accessed 2 February 2010]

European Commission (2007b) *Public financial management performance report – Dominican Republic.* November 2007 [online] ec.europa.eu/europeaid/what/economic-support/ public-finance/ documents/domrepublic_pefa en.pdf [Accessed 2 February 2010]

Fisman, R. and Gatti, R. (2002) 'Decentralization and corruption: Evidence across countries' [online] wbln0018.worldbank/ research/workpapers.nsf/view+to+link+webpages/01f479d57 03058d3852568a4006952e4?opendocument [Accessed 12 July 2010]

Fjeldstad, O. (2004) 'Decentralization and corruption: A review of the literature', Chr. Michelsen Institute, CMI Working Paper WP 2004:10

Friedman, M. (1995) 'From outcomes to budgets: An approach to outcome-based budgeting for family and children services," Child Protection Clearinghouse, Center for the Study of Social Policy, Washington DC, 1995 [online] www.financeproject.org

Fritzen, S.A. and Lim, W.O. (2006) 'Problems and prospects of decentralization in developing countries' [online] www.spp.nus. edu.sg/docs/wp/wp16_06.pdf [Accessed 21 January 2012]

Gonzales de Anis (2000) 'Reducing corruption at the local level', World Bank Institute [online] www.anti-corr.ru/archive/reducing% 20corruption%20at%20the%20local%20level.pdf [Accesses 6 August 2010]

Gonzalez, E.T. (2007) 'Policy transfer in the Philippines: Can it pass the localization test?'*JOAAG*, vol.2 (1), pp.1-10

Goldsmith, E., 'Institutions in crisis [online] www.rsesymposia.org/themedia/file/1151633172-crisis.pdf [Accessed 12 November 2010]

Gurgur, T. and Shah, A. (2000) 'Localization and Corruption: Panacea or Pandora's Box?' [online] www.imf.org/external/ pubs/ft/ seminar/ 2000/fiscal/gurgur.pdf [Accessed 12 July 2010]

Haque, M.S. (2007) 'Revisiting the New Public Management', *Public Administration Review*, January/February 2007, pp.179-182

Haque, M.S. (1997) 'Local governance in developing nations: Re-examining the question of accountability', *Regional Development Dialogue*, vol.18 (2), pp.iii-xxiii

Heilbrunn, J.R. (2004) 'Anti-corruption commissions: Panacea or real medicine to fight corruption?', World Bank Institute [online] www.sitesources.worldbank.org/wbi/resources/wbi37234heil brunn.pdf [Accessed 1 August 2010]

Hood, C. (1991) 'A public management for all seasons?'*Public Administration*, vol.69, Spring 1991, pp.3-19

Howlett, M. and Ramesh, M. (2003) *Studying public policy: Policy cycles and policy subsystems*, Oxford: Oxford University Press

Hudson, J. and Lowe, S. (2004) *Understanding the policy process: Analysis welfare policy and practice*, Bristol: Polity Press

Jacobsson, B. and Sundtrom, G. (2007) 'Governing state agencies: Transformations in the Swedish administrative model' [online] regulation.upf.edu/ecpr-07-papers/ bjacobsson.pdf [Accessed 17 March 2011]

James, O. and Lodge, M. (2003) 'The limitations of 'policy transfer' and 'lesson drawing' for public policy research', *Political Studies Review*, vol.1, pp.179-193

Karingi, S.N. (2003) 'Fiscal policy and growth in Africa: Fiscal federalism, decentralization and incidence of taxation. Theoretical and practical issues in decentralization and fiscal devolution: Lessons from and for Kenya', *United Nations Economic Commission for Africa Ad-Hoc Expert Group Meeting*, 7-9 October 2003 [online] www.uneca.org/eca. resources/meetings _events/espd/fiscal/ papers/formatted_karingi.pdf [Accessed 12 July 2010]

Karna, S.K. (2011) 'International conference on decentralization, local governance and service delivery: Sharing experience and sustaining progress in urban Iraq' *Position Paper*, UN-Habitat Iraq Programme[online]www.unhabitat.org/downloads/ doc/9575_ 41579_iraq_event2011.pdf [Accessed 30 June 2011]

Keller-Herzog, A. (2006) 'Advocacy and legal advice centers project brief', Transparency International, file 'ALAC_Project_ Brief[1]. doc' [online] www.transparency.org/regional_pages/ europe _ central_asia/priority_issues#priority3 [Accessed 27 July 2010]

Kerr, S. (1975) 'On the folly of rewarding A, while hoping for B', *Academy of Management Journal* (December 1975), vol.18 (4), pp.769-783

Klitgaard, R. (1998) 'International cooperation against corruption', *Finance and Development* (March 1998), pp.3-6

Klitgaard, R., MacLean-Abaroa, R. and Parris, H. (2000) *Corrupt cities: A practical guide to cure and prevention*, ICS Press and World Bank [online] books.google.com/books?id=Bju8SS6m MjgC&printsec =frontcover&dq=Klitgaard i Corrupt+cities+2000&source=bl& ots=G5K-gYE20a&sig=UmJ-TaqLVURyFXgcjBbvjpOhes&hl= en&ei=7U1cTNaBNJH4sAOetJjQAQ&sa=X&oi=book_result

&ct=result&resnum=1&ved=0CBIQ6AEwAA#v=onepage&q =Klitgaard%20Corrupt%20cities%202000&f=false[Accessed 6 August 2010]

Ik-Sik Kim, I.S. (2007), 'Strategies for regional development thru citizen participation' [online] www.clg.uts.edu.au/pdfs/ iksikkimpresenta tion.pdf [Accessed 17 June 2011]

Kurer, O. (2005) 'Corruption: An alternative approach to its definition and measurement', *Political Studies*, vol.53, pp.222-239

Kwok, T.M-W (2006) 'Formulating an effective anti-corruption strategy – The experience of Hong Kong ICAC, Resource Material Series No.69 [online] www.unafei.or.jp/english/pdf/pdf_rms/no69/ 16_p196-201.pdf [Accessed 1 August 2010]

Ladi, S. (1999) 'Globalization, think tanks and policy transfer', Paper presented at the World Bank Conference of the Global Development Network, Bonn, Germany, 5-9 December 1999 [online] citeseerx.ist.psu.edu/viewdoc/download?doi=10.1.1.4 0.5748[1].pdf [Accessed on 24 May 2010]

Lee, R.D. and Johnson, R.W. (1994) *Public budgeting systems*, 5th ed. Gaithersburg: Aspen Publisher Inc.

Lewis, S. (2005) *Race against time*. Toronto: House of Anansi Press Inc.

MacCarthaigh, M. (2010) 'Where do agencies go when they die? A longitudinal analysis of agency termination' [online] egpa2010. com/documents/PSG6/Muiris_MacCarthaigh_EGPA% 202010. pdf [Accessed 17 March 2011]

Marsh, D. and Smith, M. (2000) 'Understanding policy networks: Towards a dialectical approach', *Political Studies*, vol.48 (1), pp.4-21

Mauro, P. (1998) 'Corruption: Causes, consequences, and agenda for further research', *Finance and Development* (March 1998), pp.11-14

McCarthy, P. (2005) 'Drivers of change: An evaluation of the Advocacy and Legal Advice Centers project', Transparency International, file 'ALAC_Final_Evaluation_Report_2005 [1].doc' [online] www.transparency.org/regional_pages/europe_central_asia/ priority_issues#priority3 [Accessed 27 July 2010]

Melaville, A.I. (1997) 'A guide to selecting results and indicators: Implementing results-based budgeting', May 1997 [online] www.financeproject.org

Merton, R.K. (1940) 'Bureaucratic structure and personality', *Social Forces*, vol.18 (4), May 1940, pp.560-568

Moynihan, D.P. (2006) 'Ambiguity in policy lessons: The agencification experience' [online] www.lafollette.wisc.edu/facultystaff/ moyhinan/ pa06ambiguity.pdf [Accessed 17 March 2011]

Nedley, A. (2004) 'Policy transfer and the developing country experience gap: Taking a southern perspective.' In Evans, M. (ed.) *Policy transfer in global perspective*, Aldershot: Ashgate Publishing Limited. Pp.165-189 [online] books.google.com/books?id= mlR KdrwOWbgC&pg=PA165&dq=anthony+nedley&cd=1#v=onep age&q=anthony%20nedley&f=false [Accessed 24 May 2010]

Norwegian Agency for Development Cooperation - Norad (2008) *Public Financial Management Performance Report – Norway.* Norad Report 15/2008 [online] www.norad.no/en/Tools+and+ publications/publications/publication+page?key=109797 [Accessed 1 February 2010]

Nunan, F. (1999) 'Policy Network Transformation: The Implementation of the EC Directive on Packaging and Packaging Waste', Public Administration, vol.77 (3), pp.621-638

Obama, B.H. (2010) *State of the Union Address* [online] www.cnn.com/2010/politics/01/27/sotu.transcropt/index.html ?section=cnn_latest [Accessed 27 January 2010]

Oduwaye, L. (2006) 'Effects of Globalization on Cities in Developing Countries', *Journal of Social Sciences*, vol.12 (3), pp.199-205

Organisation for Economic Co-operation and Development – OECD (2005) *Economic Survey of Australia, 2004.* Policy Brief, January 2005 [online] www.oedc.org/dataoecd/12/51/34333216.pdf [Accessed 3 February 2010]

Organisation for Economic Co-operation and Development – OECD (2002) *Next steps for public spending in New Zealand: The pursuit of effectiveness.* Economic Department Working Papers No. 337, August 2002 [online] www.olis.oecd.org/olis/2002doc.nfs/linkto /nt00002996/$file/jt00130148.pdf [Accessed 1 February 2010]

Organisation for Economic Co-operation and Development – OECD (1999) *Coping with population ageing in Australia.* Economic Department Working Papers No. 217, July 1999 [online] www.oecd.org/dataoecd/ 0/19/1879131.pdf [Accessed 3 February 2010]

Page, E.C. (2000) 'Future governance and the literature on policy transfer and lesson drawing', [online] www.hull.ac.uk/futgov/papers/ edpagepaper.pdf [Accessed 24 May 2010]

Peck, J. and Theodore, N. (2001) 'Exporting workfare/importing welfare-to-work: Exploring the politics of Third Way policy transfer', *Political Geography*, vol.20, pp.427-460

Perrin, B. (2002) 'Implementing the vision: Addressing challenges to results-focused management and budgeting', Paper presented to OECD meeting of 11-12 February 2002, Paris [online] www.oecd.org/dataoecd/4/10/2497163.pdf [Accesses 11 November 2010]

Pierson, C. (2003) 'Learning from Labor? Welfare policy transfer between Australia and Britain', *Commonwealth & Comparative Politics*, vol.41 (1), pp.77-100

Quah, J.S.T. 'Combating corruption in Singapore: What can be learned?'*Journal of Contingencies and Crisis Management* (March 2001), vol.9 (1), pp.29-35

Reinikka, R. and Svensson, J. (2003) 'The power of information: Evidence from a newspaper campaign to reduce capture', [online] www.wds.worldbank.org/servlet/wdsconentserver/wdsp/ib/2004/03/26/000012009_20040326142036/rendered/pdf/wps3239.pdf [Accessed 27 July 2010]

Rizvi, G. (2007) "Reinventing government: Putting democracy and social justice back into the disclosure." In United Nations Department of Economic and Social Development (*e.d.*) *Public administration and democratic governance: Government serving citizens*. New York: United Nations Publications

Robertson-Snape, F. (1999) 'Corruption, collusion and nepotism in Indonesia', *Third World Quarterly*, vol.20 (3), pp.589-602

Rose, R. (1991) 'What is Lesson-Drawing?'*Journal of Public Policy*, vol.11 (1), pp.3-30

Rubin, I.S. (2000) 'The politics of public budgets,' in Stillman's *Public administration: Concepts and cases, Seventh Edition*, Boston: Houghton Mifflin Company, p.376

Saldanha, C., Regional and Sustainable Development Department, *The Governance Brief* [online] www.adb.org/governance

Scheers, B., Sterk, M. and Bouckaert, G. (2005) 'Lessons from Australian and British reforms in results-oriented financial management' *OECD Journal on Budgeting*, 5 (2): 134-162 [online] www.oecd. org/dataoecd/4/51/43480984.pdf [Accessed 3 February 2010]

Schick, A. (1998) *A contemporary approach to public expenditure management.* Washington: World Bank Institute [online] www1. worldbank.org/publicsector/pe/PEM_book.pdf [Accessed 14 February 2010]

Segal, L. (1997) 'The pitfalls of political decentralization and proposals for reform: The case of New York City public schools', *Public Administration Review*, March/April 1997, vol.57 (2), pp.141-149

Shah, A. (1998) 'Balance, accountability, and responsiveness: Lessons from decentralization', World Bank, *Policy Research Working Paper 2021* (December 1998)

Stone, D. (2000) 'Non-governmental policy transfer: The strategies of independent policy institutions', *Governance: An International Journal of Policy and Administration*, vol.13 (1), pp.45-62

Stone, D. (1999) 'Learning lessons and transferring policy across time, space and disciplines', *Politics*, vol.19 (1), pp.51-59

Stribu, M. (2008) 'Monitoring and evaluation, knowledge management, and public policy – the x, y and z of the Millennium Development Goals equation' In UNICEF (2008) 'Evaluation: South Asia' [online] www.unicef.org/rosa/ROSA_Evaluation_Journal.pdf [Accessed 12 November 2010]

Sulle, A.S. (2008) 'Executive agencies in Tanzania: A descriptive analysis' [online] soc.kuleven.be/io/cost/act/paper/2008/Tanzania _sulle. doc [Accessed 17 March 2011]

Talbot, C. (2003) 'Measuring public value: A competing values approach' [online] www.workfoundation.co.uk/assets/docs/measuring_pv _fianl 2.pdf [Accessed 8 April 2011]

Talbot, C. and Pollitt, C. (2000) 'The idea of Agency: Researching the agencification of the (public service) world' [online] www.uned. es/113016/docencia/spd%20doctorado%202001-02/ agencias/ talbot%20et%20al.%20agency%20apsa%202000.pdf [Accessed 17 March 2011]

Tarallo, M.A. (2012) *Valuing people: citizen engagement in policy making and public service delivery in rural Asia*, Bloomington: AuthorHouse

Tarallo, M.A. (2004) *UN budgeting: A sound leap forward*, Bloomington: AuthorHouse

Tiebout, C.M. (1956) 'A pure theory of local expenditures', *The Journal of Political Economy*, vol.64 (5), pp.416-424

Treisman, D. (2000) 'Decentralization and the quality of government', University of California [online] www.imf.org/external/pubs /ft/ seminar/2000/fiscal/treisman.pdf [Accessed 12 July 2010]

United Nations (2010) [online] www.un.org/millenniumgoals [Accessed 12 November 2010]

United Nations (2004a) *United Nations Convention Against Corruption*, General Assembly Resolution 58/4 of 31 October 2003

United Nations (2004b) *United Nations handbook on practical anti-corruption measures for prosecutors and investigators*, United

Nations Office on Drugs and Crime, Vienna, (September 2004)

United Nations (2004c) Department of Economic and Social Development, *Public administration country profile – Ethiopia.* June 2004 [online] unpan1.un.org/intradoc/groups/ public/ documents/public/un/unpan023264.pdf [Accessed 1 February 2010]

United Nations (2004d) Department of Economic and Social Development,*Public administration country profile – The Philippines.* February 2004 [online] unpan1.un.org/intradoc/ groups/public/documents/public/un/unpan023241.pdf [Accessed 1 February 2010]

United States Department of the Treasury (2010) Treasury budget focused on building new foundation for economic growth, reform of the financial system [online] www.realestaterama. com/2010/02/01/ treasury-budget-focused-on-building-new-foundation-for-economic-growth-reform-of-the-financial-system-id06548.html [Accessed 2 February 2010]

United Nations Development Programme – UNDP (1997) 'Corruption and good governance', *Discussion Paper 3* [online] www.un.org. kg/ en/publications/document-database/article/document-database/un-system-in-kyrgyzstan/human-rights-and-human-rights-based-approach/115-overnance/2140-undp-corruption-and-good-governance-eng.pdf [Accessed 2 August 2010]

University of Birmingham (2010a) *Governance*, School of Government and Society. International Development Department

University of Birmingham (2010b) *Making Policy*, School of Government and Society. International Development Department

Vabo, M. (2009) 'New Public Management: The neoliberal way of governance' [online] www.ts.hi.is/working%20paper%204-2009.pdf [Accessed 24 March 2011]

van Thiel, S. and CRIPO - Comparative Research into Current Trends in Public Sector Organization (2009) 'The rise of executive agencies: Comparing the agencification of 25 tasks in 21 countries' [online] soc.kuleuven.be/io/egpa/org/2009malta/papers/egpa%202009%20thiel%20the%20rise%executive%20agencies.pdf [Accessed 17 March 2001]

Walker, M.B.L. (2009) 'Left behind in the loopholes: An examination of bureaucratic goal displacement', Paper prepared for the 2009 Annual Meeting of the Midwest Political Science Association, 2-5 April 2009 [online] www.allacademic.com/meta/p362361_index.html [Accessed 11 November 2010]

Walsh, K. (1995), *Public Services and Market mechanisms: Competition, Contracting Out and the New Public Management*, Basingstoke: Macmillan

Warner, W.K. and Havens, A.E. (1968) 'Goal displacement and the intangibility of organizational goals', *Administrative Science Quarterly*, (Mar. 1968), vol.12(4), pp.539-555

World Bank (2009) Gross Domestic Product 2008 [online] siteresources.worldbank.org/datastatistics/resources/gdp.pdf [Accessed 7 February 2010]

World Bank (2003a) *Country financial accountability assessment – Antigua & Barbuda, Dominica, Grenada, St. Kitts & Nevins, St. Lucia, St. Vincent & The Grenadines*. April 2003 [online] www.unpan.org/library/fulltextsearch/tabid/1089/language/en-us/default.aspx [Accessed 2 February 2010).

World Bank (2003b) *Country financial accountability assessment – Ethiopia.Vol. I Main report.* September 2003 [online] www-wds. worldbank.org/external/default/WDSContentServer/WDSP/ IB/2003/09/30/000160016_20030930104011/Rendered/PDF/ 260921 ETvol01.pdf [Accessed 7 February 2010]

World Bank (2003c) *Improving government performance: Discipline, efficiency and equity in managing public resources – Philippines.* April 2003 [online] www-wds.worldbank.org/external/default/ WDSContentServer/WDSP/IB/2003/07/25/000094946_030717 04132781/Rendered/PDF/multi0page.pdf [Accessed 3 February 2010]

World Bank (2001) 'Decentralization and governance: Does decentralization improve public service delivery?'*PremNotes* No. 55, June 2001

Yamamoto, H. (2003) 'New Public Management – Japan's practice' [online] www.iips. org/bp293e.pdf [Accessed 24 March 2011]

Yeung, J.A. (2000) 'Fighting corruption: The Hong Kong experience' [online] www.tdri.or.th/ reports/unpublished/ospaper/auyeung .pdf [Accessed 28 July 2010]

Youde, J. (2005) 'South Africa, AIDS, and the development of counter-epistemic community', Paper prepared for presentation at the 2005 International Studies Association Conference, Honolulu, Hawaii, 1-5 March 2005 [online] cyber.law.harvard.edu/blogs/ gems/ politicshiv/youde.pdf [Accessed 9 June 2010]

Zuleta, J.C., Leyton, A. and Ivanovic, R.F. (2008) 'Corruption in the revenue service: The case of VAT refunds in Bolivia' [online] www1.worldbank.org/publicsector/ taxcorruptioncase.doc [Accessed 1 August 2010]

ABOUT THE AUTHOR

Michael Anthony Tarallo is an international civil servant, whose career in international financial management spans 22 years. He has served in the United States, Austria, Kosovo, Israel, and Darfur, with special assignments in Jordan and Cyprus. He holds masters in political science and public administration and development. He is currently in charge of the financial resources for the United Nations peacekeeping mission in Darfur, currently the largest both in terms of funding and personnel.

He was born in New York and relocated to Rome, Italy, where he spent his childhood and teenage formative years. The international character of both his family- and professionally-driven relocations has allowed him to meet people from all walks of life and appreciate wide ranging cultures, customs, and traditions.

He has authored also *Valuing People: Citizen Engagement in Policy Making and Public Service Delivery in Rural Asia* (2012) and *UN Budgeting: A Sound Leap Forward* (2004).

He is married and a proud father of three children.